"it's mainly because of the meat" and other recipes

COOKBOOK

from  **Dominion**

Recipes tested and approved by

Joan Fielden

Dominion Stores Limited
Food Consultant

edited by
E. D. HARVISON

Printed in Canada
by
Sampson Matthews Ltd., Don Mills, Ont.

Copies of this book may be obtained through
Dominion Stores Limited, 605 Rogers Road, Toronto, Ont. M6M 1B9

Table of Contents

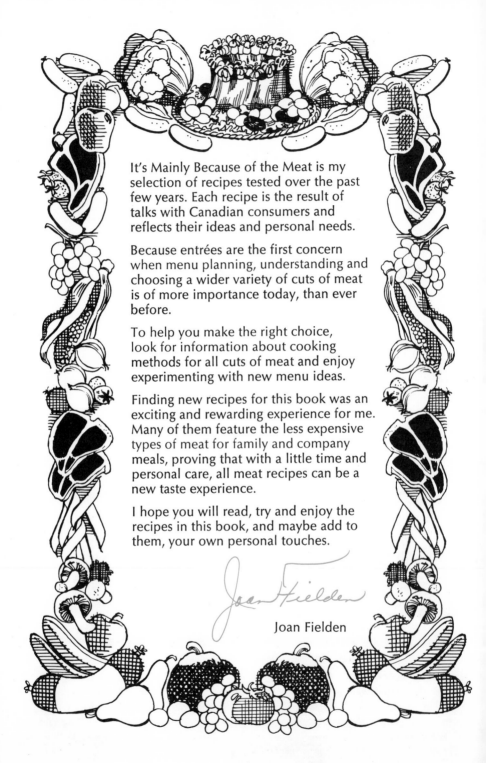

It's Mainly Because of the Meat is my selection of recipes tested over the past few years. Each recipe is the result of talks with Canadian consumers and reflects their ideas and personal needs.

Because entrées are the first concern when menu planning, understanding and choosing a wider variety of cuts of meat is of more importance today, than ever before.

To help you make the right choice, look for information about cooking methods for all cuts of meat and enjoy experimenting with new menu ideas.

Finding new recipes for this book was an exciting and rewarding experience for me. Many of them feature the less expensive types of meat for family and company meals, proving that with a little time and personal care, all meat recipes can be a new taste experience.

I hope you will read, try and enjoy the recipes in this book, and maybe add to them, your own personal touches.

Joan Fielden

Tips on Buying and Cooking Meats.

QUANTITY TO BUY

The total amount of meat to buy depends upon the number of persons to be served and whether you wish to have sufficient left over for another meal. The following guide will be useful:

Boneless meat — ¼ pound per serving.

Bone-in meat — ½ pound per serving.

Bony meat — ¾ to 1 pound per serving.

Plan on 2 to 3 servings for hearty appetites. Plan leftovers for big cuts requiring long cooking. Refer to the storage time charts for assistance in planning the quantity of leftover meat.

COOK-BY-THE-BOOK

There are only two basic methods in cooking meat: dry heat and moist heat. Within each category there are variations:

Dry Heat	Moist Heat
Roasting	Braising
Broiling	Cooking in water
Pan-broiling	Stewing
Pan-frying	Pressure cooking
Rotisserie	

Beef may be served rare, medium, or well-done, depending on the taste choice of your family. Serve lamb medium or well-done. Veal is best served well-done. Pork should **always** be well-done. Use a meat thermometer for accuracy.

How To Use a Meat Thermometer: Insert the point of the meat thermometer into the center of the thickest part of the meat, not touching bone. The thermometer will register the **internal** temperature of the meat and the dial readings will tell you when your roast is cooked the way you want it. Do not use a thermometer except when roasting meat.

ROASTING

Place meat, fat side up, on a rack in an open pan. Do not cover, do not add water, do not baste. Cook in a slow oven (325°F.) until done. Use a meat thermometer if possible.

BROILING

Steaks and chops should be at least 1 inch thick; ham slices should be ½ inch thick. Preheat broiler. Slash fat at edge at 1 inch intervals being very careful not to cut into meat. This prevents meat from curling as it cooks. Place meat on rack in broiling pan. Place 1 inch steaks or chops 2 to 3 inches from heat; 2 inch cuts 3 to 5 inches from heat. Broil until nicely browned. Turn over and broil other side. Turn only once and use tongs. If you must use a fork, insert it in the fat, not the meat.

PAN-BROILING

Preheat a heavy skillet and rub it with some meat fat to prevent sticking. Slash fat on steaks and chops at 1 inch intervals to prevent curling. Brown meat on both sides, then reduce temperature to complete cooking if necessary. Do not cover. Do not add water. Pour off fat as it accumulates.

PAN-FRYING

Pan fry meats low in natural fat such as round steak, liver, veal steaks and chops, etc. Place **small** amount of fat in pan and heat to almost smoking. Brown meat quickly and then reduce heat and cook, uncovered until meat is done.

ROTISSERIE ROASTING

Let roast come to room temperature. Slip holding fork on rod; push rod through **center** of roast, inserting tines of holding fork firmly into meat. Push in the second holding fork and fasten. Cradle the ends of the rod in your upturned hands and rotate the roast. If it spins easily, fine. If not it **must** be remounted. When it spins to your satisfaction tighten the fork screws with pliers. A meat thermometer is a must; but make sure its point does not touch fat, bone or the metal spit.

BRAISING

Coat meat in seasoned flour if desired. Brown slowly on all sides in hot fat. Season with salt and pepper, herbs or spices. Add a **very small** amount of liquid to prevent sticking. Cover tightly. Turn heat to low to simmer on range top or place in 325°F. oven.

COOKING IN WATER

Cover meat with **cold** water and bring just to boil. Skim until foam stops rising. Add seasonings such as bay leaf, onions, celery tops, etc. and turn down heat until liquid "smiles" (a bubble bursts on the surface about every 10 seconds or so). Cover tightly and cook until meat is fork tender. See recipes for approximate times.

STEWING

Cut meat in uniform pieces, usual 1 to 2 inch cubes. Coat with seasoned flour and brown slowly in hot fat. Add herbs and spices called for. Add approximately 1 cup of liquid (water, bouillon, tomato juice or mixture). Let liquid "smile" (as described above) until meat is tender. Vegetables may be added during last 40 minutes of cooking. Thicken liquid to make gravy if desired.

PRESSURE COOKING

Follow the instructions which each manufacturer includes with the appliance.

BEEF CHART

RETAIL CUTS

WHOLESALE CUTS

DIAGRAM OF CUTTING

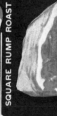

ROUND

STEAK PIECE OR SIRLOIN BUTT

ROUND RUMP ROAST

SQUARE RUMP ROAST

PORTERHOUSE ROAST

ROUND STEAK

SIRLOIN STEAK

WING OR CLUB STEAK

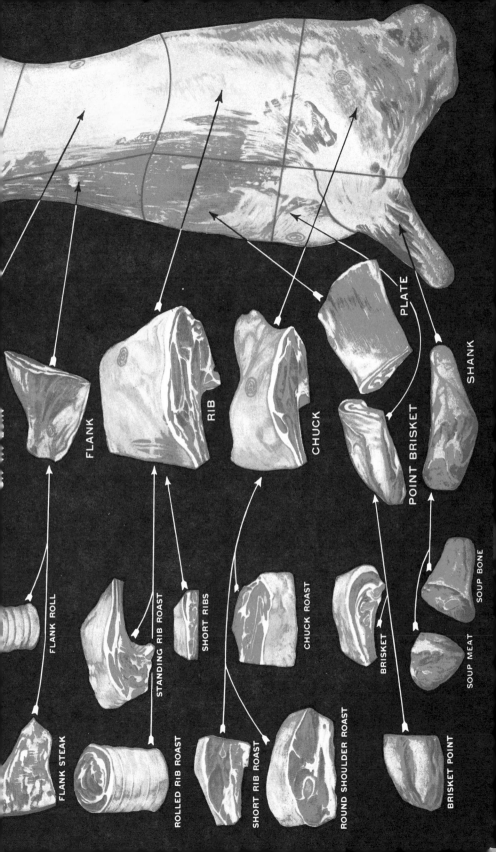

FLANK

RIB

CHUCK

PLATE

POINT BRISKET

SHANK

FLANK ROLL

STANDING RIB ROAST

SHORT RIBS

CHUCK ROAST

BRISKET

SOUP BONE

SOUP MEAT

FLANK STEAK

ROLLED RIB ROAST

SHORT RIB ROAST

ROUND SHOULDER ROAST

BRISKET POINT

FROM STORE TO STORAGE

It is necessary to wrap meat properly before storing. You have invested money—now invest a few minutes of time. Unwrap fresh meat and place in the meat compartment. If you don't have a special compartment, place meat on a plate and cover loosely with waxed paper, box or plastic film. Follow storage time chart.

Leftover meat should be cooled and refrigerated in a covered dish.

REFRIGERATOR STORAGE TIME CHART
Temperature 36° to 40°F. or 2°C to 5°C

MEAT	Limit of Days for Maximum Quality
BEEF	
Roasts	5 to 8 days
Steaks	3 to 5 days
Pot Roasts	5 to 6 days
Stew Meat, Ground Meat, Liver, Heart	2 days
PORK	
Roasts	5 to 6 days
Chops and Spareribs	3 days
Sausage	2 to 3 days
LAMB	
Roasts	5 days
Chops	3 days
Heart, Liver	2 days
VEAL	
Roasts	5 to 6 days
Chops	4 days
Liver, Sweetbreads (cooked)	2 days
CURED AND SMOKED MEATS	
Hams, Picnics (whole or half)	7 days
Ham slices	3 days
Bacon	5 to 7 days
Dried Beef	10 to 12 days
Corned Beef	5 to 7 days
Tongue	6 to 7 days
COOKED MEATS	
Home-cooked Meats	4 days
Hams, Picnics	7 days
Wieners	4 to 5 days
"Cold Cuts"	3 days

Tips on Freezing Food

- Package meat tightly in moisture-vapourproof wrapping or container especially made for freezer storage. A good wrap helps prevent "freezer burn", keeps meat juicy, flavourful. Packaged self-service meats may be frozen in original store package if there are no breaks in the package.

- Mark each package or container with the name of the meat; the number of pieces or servings for chops, short ribs, etc.; and the date, so the meat will be used within the accepted storage time.

- Freeze meat at 0°F or less. The faster meat freezes, the better the quality will be retained. Use meats as soon as is practical after freezing — they don't improve with age.

- Roasts and stew meats may be boned and all excess fat removed to save storage space.

- Thawing and refreezing is not desirable because it gives an opportunity for increased bacterial action.

- Do not soak unwrapped meat in water to hasten thawing. This impairs flavour because of loss of juices.

- Meat wrapped in moisture-proof paper may be thawed in cold water.

FREEZER STORAGE TIME CHART*

For meats stored in a household freezer at 0°C -17.8°C or lower.

Beef ....10 to 12 months

Fresh pork and veal ....4 to 5 months

Lamb ....6 to 7 months

Ground Meat, Variety Meats† ....3 to 4 months

Smoked hams, picnic slab bacon ....3 to 6 weeks

Fresh pork sausage, bologna,
    sliced bacon, frankfurters ....Do not freeze

Chicken (ready to cook) ....6 to 12 months

Turkey (ready to cook) ....6 to 12 months

Cooked chicken and turkey ....2 to 3 months

Cooked meats, stews, meat loaves ......1 to 2 months

Gravy (unthickened) ....3 to 4 months

*This chart gives storage times for properly wrapped meats of good quality, held not more than 10 days as fresh meat before freezing. Times given are limit for top quality.

†Liver...freeze uncooked
Sweetbreads.....................................cooked
Tongues (can be frozen fresh but better to have them corned or smoked)
Brains..cooked or uncooked
Hearts.. uncooked
Kidney ....uncooked
Tripe .... cooked
Oxtails..uncooked

ROASTING
TEMPERATURE AND TIME CHART

Beef Cut	Oven Temperature	Minutes Per Pound	Internal Meat Temperature
Standing Rib (3) ...	300°-325°F.	18-20 rare 22-25 medium 27-30 well done	140°F. rare 160°F. medium 170°F. well done
Rolled Rib	300°-325°F.	30-32 rare 35-38 medium 40-45 well done	140°F. rare 160°F. medium 170°F. well done
Chuck Rib	300°-325°F.	25-30	150°-170°F.
Rump	300°-325°F.	20-22 rare 25-30 medium	150°-170°F. R 150°-170°F. M
Rolled Rump	300°-325°F.	30-35 rare 35-40 medium 40-45 well done	130°-140°F. R 140°-150°F. M 150°-160°F. WD
Porterhouse Roast, Wing, T-bone or Sirloin	325°F	20-22 rare 25-30 medium 30-35 well done	130°-140°F. R 140°-150°F. M 150°-160°F. WD
Round	325°F	25-30 medium	150°-160°F. M
Whole Tenderloin .	300°-325°F.	25 rare 30-35 medium	140°F. R 160°F. M
Loin	300°F.	18-20 rare 22-25 medium 27-30 well done	140°F. R 160°F. M 170°F. WD
Fillet (whole)......	325°F	never more than 40 minutes	140°F. R 160°F. M

Note 1: For searing method, cook at 450°F. for 20 minutes, then at 300° for
16 - 18 minutes per pound rare.
18 - 22 minutes per pound medium
23 - 28 minutes per pound well done.

Note 2: To cook frozen roasts, thawed; cook as fresh.
unthawed; increase cooking time by half that required for fresh.

Note 3: Large roasts require a little less cooking time per pound than small roasts.

13

ROAST LAMB	Oven Temperature	Minutes Per Pound	Internal Meat Temperature
Roast of Lamb—			
Boneless	325°F.	35 - 45	175° - 180°F.
Bone-in	325°F.	30 - 35	175° - 180°F.

Note: To cook frozen roasts, thawed, cook as fresh.
To cook frozen roasts, unthawed, increase cooking time by half.

ROAST VEAL	Oven Temperature	Time Per Pound	Internal Meat Temperature
Roast of Veal—			
Boneless	325°F.	45 - 50 min.	170° - 180°F.
Bone-in	325°F.	35 - 40 min.	170° - 180°F.

Note: To cook frozen roasts, thawed, cook as fresh.
To cook frozen roasts, unthawed, increase cooking time by half.
Boned roasts require more time than roasts with bones.

ROAST PORK	Oven Temperature	Minutes Per Pound	Internal Meat Temperature
Fresh Pork—			
Boneless	350°F.	40 - 50	185°F.
Bone-In	350°F.	30 - 35	185°F.
Cured, uncooked ...	300°F.	25 - 30	165° - 170°F.
Cured and Smoked uncooked	325°F.	20 - 25	165° - 170°F.
Smoked, fully cooked	Check cooking instructions on label		

Notes: Pork should be well done.
Picnic Shoulders and Cottage Rolls can be cooked in roast pan with ½ cup water.
To cook frozen roasts, thawed, cook as fresh.
To cook frozen roasts, unthawed, increase cooking time by half the time required for fresh pork.

BROILED BEEF STEAKS

Because steaks vary in size, shape, amount of bone and fat, etc., broiling times are only approximate. Decrease or increase broiling time to suit individual taste.

| | Minutes Each Side | | |
	Rare	Medium	Well Done
½ inch steak	1½ - 2	2 - 2½	2½ - 3
1 inch steak	5 - 7	7 - 9	9 - 11
2 inch steak	12 - 16	16 - 18	18 - 21
1 inch Filet Mignon	5	6 - 7	7 - 9
Ground Patties (1" x 3") . .	5 - 7	7 - 10	10 - 15

Note 1: Test for doneness—cut slit in meat near bone, see if colour of meat inside is of desired rareness.

Note 2: To broil frozen steaks—thaw—broil as fresh unthawed—preheat broiler 5 minutes; place steak on cold broiler pan 7 inches from heating unit; heat steak until thawed (1-inch steak 7 - 8 minutes each side). Raise broiler pan and broil as for a fresh steak.

Note 3: For steaks over 2 inches, sear each side then cook at 350°F. for 20 minutes each side; test both sides, cook longer if necessary.

PAN-BROILED STEAK

T-bone, Club, Sirloin, Rib, Porterhouse, Top of Round, ½ - ¾-inch thick.
- Brown both sides; cook 10 minutes each side or until desired doneness.
Hamburg Steaks (1-inch)—4 - 8 minutes. Minute Steaks, ¼ - ½-inch thick.
- Brown both sides; cook 2 - 3 minutes each side or until desired doneness.

PAN-FRY STEAK

- Brown over high heat 1 minute each side, cook over moderate heat.

| | Minutes Per Side | | |
	Rare	Medium	Well Done
½-inch	1 - 2	2 - 3	3 - 4
1-inch	3 - 4	4 - 5	5 - 6

PAN-FRY FROZEN STEAKS

| | Minutes Per Side | | |
	Rare	Medium	Well Done
½-inch	3 - 4	4 - 6	6 - 7
1-inch	9 - 11	11 - 12	12 - 13

SWISS STEAK

- Pan-fry 15 minutes and then stew for 2 hours.

POT ROASTING TIMETABLE

	Minutes Per Pound	
	Top of Stove	325°F. Oven
Bone-in	25 - 30	30 - 35
Boneless	30 - 35	35 - 40
OR As Per Recipe Directions		

Note 1: Allow longer times per pound for 3 - 6 pound roasts and shorter times for 6 - 8 pound roasts.

Note 2: To cook frozen pot roasts, thawed—cook as fresh.
Unthawed—brown frozen cuts well and increase cooking time by one half that required for fresh.

Note 3: To pressure cook—brown pot roast on all sides; season, add ¼ cup water. At 15 pounds pressure cook 12 - 15 minutes per pound.
To pressure cook frozen pot roasts; thawed, cook as fresh; unthawed, brown frozen cuts well and increase cooking time by ¼ that required for fresh.

ROAST POULTRY CHART

Roast Poultry	Weight (lbs.)	Oven Temp.	Total Roasting Time (hrs.)	Internal Meat Temp.
Broilers, Fryers	1½ - 2½	325°F	1½ - 2	190 - 200°F
Capon	6 - 9	325°F	2½ - 4	200°F
Chickens, roasting . .	3½ - 6	325°F	2 - 3½	190 - 200°F
Cornish Game Hens	1 - 1½	375°F - 400°F	1¼	200°F
Duck	4 - 6	350°F	2 - 2½	
Goose	8 - 12	325°F	3 - 4	
Guinea Hen	2 - 2½	350°F	1¼ - 1¾	
Pheasant	1 - 3	350°F - 375°F	1 - 1½	
Squab	1½	350°F - 375°F	1 - 1¼	
Turkey	7 - 9	325°F	3 - 4	195°F
Turkey, foil wrapped	8 - 10	450°F	2¼ - 2½	190°F

VARIETY MEATS — RECOMMENDED COOKING CHART

	Roast/Bake	Broil	Pan-Fry	Braise	Cook in Liquid	Pressure Cook
HEART—						15 lbs. pressure
Beef	45 min./lb.			whole 3 - 4 hrs.	3 - 4 hrs.	13 min./lb.
Veal	2 hrs./lb.			2½ - 3 hrs.	2½ - 3 hrs.	20 min./lb.
Pork	4 hrs./lb.			2½ - 3 hrs.	2½ - 3 hrs.	1 hr./lb.
Lamb	4 hrs./lb.			2½ - 3 hrs.	2½ - 3 hrs.	30 min./lb.
KIDNEY—			¼" - ½" slices 3 - 5 min.			
Beef		10 - 12 min.		Brown 325°F. 35 - 40 min.	1 - 1½ hrs.	
Veal		10 - 12 min.	½ kidney 7 - 9 min.		¾ - 1 hr.	
Pork		10 - 12 min.			¾ - 1 hr.	
Lamb		3 - 5 min./side			¾ - 1 hr.	
LIVER—				35 - 40 min. per lb.		
Beef			Brown over high heat, then 2 - 3 min. each side	slices,		
Veal slices		4 - 5 min. each side		20 - 25 min.		
Pork, whole				½ hr./lb.		
,, slices				20 - 25 min.		
Lamb		8 - 10 min.	15 min. then stew 30 min.			
TONGUE— Beef, veal, pork, lamb					3 - 4 hrs.	
TRIPE— Beef		10 - 15 min.			1½ - 2 hrs.	
SWEETBREADS		10 - 15 min. precooking in water	10 - 12 min.	20 - 25 min.	15 - 20 min.	
BRAINS		10 - 15 min. after precooking in water	13 - 16 min.	20 - 25 min.	15 - 20 min.	

SPIT ROASTING TIME AND TEMPERATURE CHART

Variety of Meat	Cut of Meat	Size or Weight	Warm-up Time for Frozen Meat		Recommended Heat of Fire*	Approximate Time for Cooking					COMMENTS
			In Refrig. to 40°F	In Room 40°-70°F		Very Rare 120°-130°	Rare 130°-135°	Med. Rare 135°-145°	Medium 145°-155°F	Well Done 155°-180°	
BEEF	Standing Rib	3-5 ribs	36-40 hrs.	8 hrs.	hot-medium	1½-2¼ hrs.	1¾-2¼ hrs.	2-2¾ hrs.	2½-3 hrs.	3-4½ hrs.	Start with very hot fire; let it burn down to medium.
	Rolled Rib	6-7 lbs.	36-40 hrs.	8 hrs.	hot-medium	1¾-2½ hrs.	2-2¾ hrs.	2¼-3 hrs.	2¾-3¼ hrs.	3¼-5 hrs.	Larded meat - longer cooking time.
	Rump	3-5 lbs.	24-30 hrs.	6 hrs.	medium	1¼-1¾ hrs.	1½-2 hrs.	1¾-2½ hrs.	2½-3 hrs.	3-4½ hrs.	
	Tenderloin (whole)	3-4 lbs.	12-18 hrs.	10 hrs.	hot	25-40 min.	35-45 min.	45-60 min.	50 min.-1¼ hrs.	1-2 hrs.	
	Sirloin	5-7 lbs.	18-24 hrs.	8 hrs.	hot-medium	1-1½ hrs.	1¼-1¾ hrs.	1¾-2¼ hrs.	2¼-3 hrs.	3-4 hrs.	Handle fire as for rib roast above.
LAMB	Leg	4-8 lbs.	15-40 hrs.	5-7 hrs.	medium	50-65 min.	1-1¼ hrs.	1¼-1½ hrs.	1½-2 hrs.	2 hrs. or more	Some believe lamb is more tender and flavoursome when cooked rare.
	Rolled Shoulder	3-6 lbs.	15-30 hrs.	4-6 hrs.	medium	50-65 min.	1-1¼ hrs.	1¼-1½ hrs.	1½-2 hrs.	2 hrs. or more	
	Ribs	4-7 lbs.	12-24 hrs.	5-6 hrs.	medium	—	¾-1 hr.	1-1¼	1¼-1½ hrs.	1¾ hrs. or more	
PORK	Loin	5-14 lbs.	28-36 hrs.	6-10 hrs.	medium	—	—	—	—	2-4 hrs.	Pork should be cooked to 185°F internal temperature.
	Shoulder	3-6 lbs.	24-30 hrs.	6-8 hrs.	medium					2-3½ hrs.	
	Fresh Ham	10-16 lbs.	30-48 hrs.	10-15 hrs.	medium					4-6 hrs.	
	Spareribs	1½-3½ lbs.	4-7 hrs.	2-3 hrs.	medium-hot					1-1½ hrs.	
	Suckling Pig	12-20 lbs.	30-54 hrs.	12-15 hrs.	medium					3-4 hrs.	
POULTRY	Chicken	3-5 lbs.	10-12 hrs.	4-5 hrs.	medium					1-1½ hrs.	Eviscerated weight. Use leg joint test for doneness.
	Turkey	10-25 lbs.	15-36 hrs.	8-10 hrs.	medium					2-4 hrs.	
	Goose	8-15 lbs.	20-30 hrs.	6-9 hrs.	medium					2-3 hrs.	
	Duckling	4-6 lbs.	13-18 hrs.	5-7 hrs.	medium					1-1½ hrs.	
VEAL	Leg	8-14 lbs.	24-36 hrs.	7-10 hrs.	medium					2-3 hrs.	
	Loin	10-13 lbs.	20-30 hrs.	6-9 hrs.	medium					1½-2½ hrs.	
	Shoulder (rolled)	3-5 lbs.	15-24 hrs.	4-6 hrs.	medium					¾-1½ hrs.	

*Hot fire, 325°F. or over; medium, 250 to 300°F.; slow, 150 to 225°F. Check with thermomet[er]

⇒METRIC IN THE KITCHEN⇐

How do I change?   What are the rules?   What are the symbols?

The following represent a guide only. There is no direct conversion for recipes but a few general rules and guidelines will help.

METRIC SYMBOLS TO REMEMBER

QUANTITY	NAME OF UNIT	SYMBOL
Temperature	degree Celsius	°C
Volume	litre	ℓ
Mass	gram kilogram	g kg
Length	metre centimetre	m cm
Energy	joule	J

*Mass (Weight) You will need to know this when shopping for meats, fruits and vegetables.

1 kg (kilogram) = 1000 g (grams) = a little more than 2 pounds.

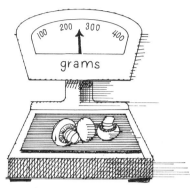 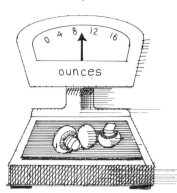

Example: **250 g** will replace 9 oz.

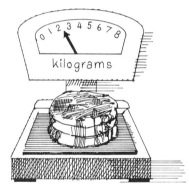 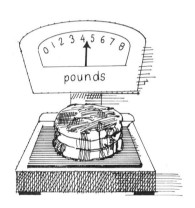

A **2 kg** roast will replace a 4.5 lb. roast.

*To most people the difference between mass and weight is not important.

Example:

1 slice of bread	= approx. **25 g**	1 apple	= approx. **150 g**
1 boiled egg	= approx. **50 g**	1 orange	= approx. **175 g**

Temperature — degrees Celsius Scale

Freezing point of water   **0°C**   32°F.
Boiling point of water   **100°C**   212°F.

A Guide to new temperature:

230°F. = **110°C**	300°F. = **149°C**	375°F. = **190°C**
250°F. = **121°C**	325°F. = **160°C**	425°F. = **220°C**
270°F. = **132°C**	350°F. = **175°C**	450°F. = **230°C**

When baking in an ovenproof glassware pan reduce temperature **10°C**.
     Refrigerator Temperature = **4°C**   Freezer Temperature = **−18°C**

DRY MEASURE
These measures are available in units of 3

50 ml *

125 ml *

250 ml *

*Actual Size

LIQUID MEASURE

Liquid measure "cup" = 250 ml.
It is graduated in 25 ml divisions.

Larger liquid measures
are 500 ml units
and 1000 ml units

These are graduated in
50 ml divisions —
1 ℓ (litre) = four 250 ml

eg: 1 glass milk = 250 ml
    1 glass juice = 125 ml

Small liquid and Dry measure: These measures are available in sets of five — 1 ml, 2 ml, 5 ml, 15 ml, 25 ml.

1 ml

2 ml

5 ml

15 ml

*Actual Size

25 ml

The 25 ml is similar to a typical coffee measure. All ingredients should be rounded up or down to nearest measure.

Conversion to metric usually involve a 5% increase in amounts. All ingredients should be rounded up or down to nearest unit.

Length

The centimetre **(cm)** slightly less than ½ inch will be a common unit for measure. In pan sizes, thickness of meat, rolled doughs, distance from broiling unit or distance between cookie sheet.

Example:

- 1 6-inch rule = **15 cm (centimetres)**
- width of little finger = **1 cm**
- 8″ x 8″ cake pan = **20 x 20 cm** (cake pan)
- Shortbreads — **1 cm** thick
- Ranges — **75 cm** wide (30″) or **60 cm** wide = (24″)
- Steak for Barbecue — **4 cm** thick (1¾″)
- Meat Balls — **3 cm** in diameter

HOT POTATO AND BEAN SOUP   Serves 6

Imperial	Metric
1 cup diced cooked ham	250 ml diced cooked ham
4 small onions, sliced	4 small onions, sliced
2 tablespoons bacon fat	50 ml bacon fat
6 medium sized diced potatoes	6 medium sized diced potatoes
1 20 ounce can red kidney beans	675 ml can red kidney beans
1 clove garlic minced	1 clove garlic minced
2 bay leaves	2 bay leaves
½ cup tomato paste	125 ml tomato paste
1 tablespoon allspice	25 ml allspice
1¼ cups consomme	300 ml consomme
¾ cups water	175 ml water

- Sauté onions in bacon fat until pale yellow, not brown.
- Add onions, kidney beans in their juice, garlic, bay leaves, potatoes and ham.
- Dilute tomato paste with consomme and water, add to meat mixture.
- Add 2 more cups of water as needed. Add 500 ml more of water as needed.
- Simmer together at least 2 hours.

MAIN MEAL OVEN ROASTS

Any of the tender cuts of beef, lamb, veal, pork and poultry may be roasted. You can use slow heat with no salt, no water, no prebrowning, no searing. This creates less shrinkage and grease-spattering than other methods. Set meat on a rack in a shallow roast pan in the centre of the oven, with fat-side up, if shape permits. When lean surface must be uppermost, spread with soft dripping to prevent drying. Use a small shallow pan for a small roast; a deep-sided large pan increases the roasting time. A shallow broiling pan may be used for large cuts, but remove the broiling grid and replace with a smaller trivet or open cake rack. Pan drippings will take on a richer colour and if basting is required, pan juices are readily accessible.

Roasting charts can give only approximate times for medium, rare, well-done, because a lean boneless roast cooks faster than a roast with bone and fat. A small roast takes more time per pound than a large roast; a thick roast takes longer than a thin roast of the same weight. For these reasons a meat thermometer is the only positive way of knowing the internal temperature regardless of weight, cut or shape of roast. Insert the metal tip into the thick centre lean muscle without resting it on bone or fat. Remove as soon as thermometer indicates the rare, medium or well-done stage. See charts for recommended cooking temperature and time for each type of roast.

Pork and veal are roasted to the well-done stage. Beef may be roasted from rare to well-done and lamb from medium to well-done. Let roast meat stand in a warm place 15 to 25 minutes before carving. Meat slices will be moister as juices stop bubbling and are re-absorbed by the meat cells. The internal temperature will rise during this standing period, so remove roast from oven when the thermometer registers 5 or 10 degrees below the "doneness" you prefer.

For oven roasting tender cuts of meat, follow times and methods in charts on pages 13 and 14. The following recipes offer interesting and flavourful variations.

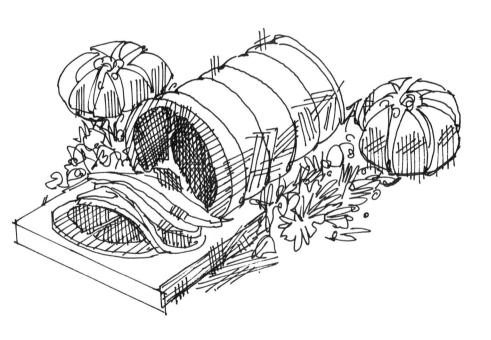

⚛ BEEF SECTION ⚛

CHARCOAL ROAST   Serves 8

4 pound rolled beef roast

Marinade

5 tablespoons Worcestershire sauce	4 tablespoons soy sauce
2 tablespoons kitchen bouquet	¾ cup olive oil
1 clove garlic, crushed	

- The rolled roast must be cut so it is flat on each end.
- Mix together the Worcestershire, kitchen bouquet, garlic, and soy sauce to make marinade. Stir well; put roast into the bowl; then rub marinade into the roast with your hands. Cover bowl; refrigerate, and let stand for at least 4 hours overnight is even better.
- When you are ready to barbecue, remove cover from bowl containing meat and marinade and pour olive oil over the roast. Again using your hands, rub meat well with the marinade and the olive oil.
- Place the roast on the grill so that it is standing on one end. Cook for about 1 hour, basting frequently with the remaining marinade and oil mixture. After a short while, it will turn black; but fear not. At the end of the hour, stand it on the other end and let continue to cook for a second hour.

FILET OF BEEF WELLINGTON

- Roast a 3-pound filet of beef in a 425°F. oven for 20 minutes.
- Allow the meat to cool thoroughly.
- Mash the contents of an 8-ounce can of pâté de foie gras; spread on all sides of the filet.
- Roll out pastry and completely enclose the meat, sealing the edges.
- Place on a baking sheet, flat side down, bake in a pre-heated 425°F oven 25 minutes, or until the pastry is browned; let stand 5 minutes before slicing.
- Serve with meat or steak sauce.

28

MARINATED BEEF

½ cup salad oil
1 cup dry red wine
1 cup sliced onion
¼ cup chopped parsley
1 bay leaf
½ teaspoon thyme

2 teaspoons salt
½ teaspoon black pepper
4 pound rump roast of beef
3 strips bacon, half cooked
and drained
1 tablespoon vinegar

- Mix together first eight ingredients.
- Marinate the meat in this mixture overnight in the refrigerator.
- Place strips of bacon on bottom of roasting pan.
- Drain meat, strain and reserve the marinade.
- Spread the vegetables on the bacon; put meat on top; add ½ cup of marinade.
- Roast in 350°F. oven for 1¾ hours, or until tender, basting frequently.
- Transfer meat to a hot serving platter and keep hot.
- Strain pan juices into saucepan, add remaining marinade; cook over high heat 5 minutes; skim off fat.
- Mix in vinegar; bring to boil; serve separately in a sauceboat.

N.B. Any roast of beef can be marinated in this manner.

ROAST BEEF WITH VEGETABLES

4 pound rib roast of beef
1 pound carrots, cut into pieces,
size of olives
1 pound string beans

6 artichoke hearts
1 pound small young peas
¾ cup butter or margarine
salt

- Roast the beef to desired degree of doneness.
- Cook each of the vegetables in lightly salted water until just tender, dress each with 2 tablespoons of butter.
- Transfer beef to a hot platter, pour off excess fat, deglaze the drippings in the pan with 2 cups wine or other acidic liquid over high heat.
- Garnish the platter with small mounds of vegetables; serve the sauce separately.

⇒VEAL SECTION⇐

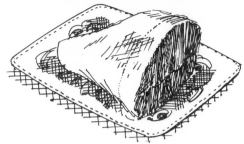

LEG OF VEAL IN TOMATO SAUCE   Serves 8 - 10

leg of veal, boned and tied	1 clove garlic, minced
2 teaspoons salt	1 28-ounce can tomatoes,
½ teaspoon black pepper	drained
2 tablespoons salad oil	1 teaspoon thyme
1 cup thinly sliced onion	3 tablespoons minced parsley

- Rub veal with salt and pepper; heat oil in a Dutch oven or heavy frying pan; brown veal on all sides.
- Add onions and garlic; cook until browned.
- Add tomatoes and thyme; cover and cook over low heat 2½ hours or until tender.
- Skim fat from the gravy and stir in parsley; remove the strings, slice veal and serve with gravy.

STUFFED SHOULDER OF VEAL   Serves 6

5 to 6 pounds veal shoulder, boned	2 tablespoons parsley, chopped
2 cloves garlic, finely chopped	10 to 12 ripe olives
1 cup dry bread crumbs, finely rolled	salt
10 anchovy fillets with oil	bacon or salt pork

- Combine garlic with bread crumbs, anchovy fillets and oil in which they are packed, parsley and ripe olives seeded and cut into slices.
- Stuff the pocket of the veal, tie securely.
- Wrap bacon or salt pork around the roast.
- Place uncovered in a 300°F. oven and cook until the roast thermometer registers 165°F. If you do not use a thermometer, allow about 35 minutes per pound for the roast.

Variations:

WITH PORK STUFFING

- Sauté 2 medium onions, finely chopped, in 3 tablespoons butter. Blend with ½ pound ground fresh pork, ½ teaspoon salt, 1 teaspoon coarse black pepper, 2 tablespoons chopped parsley, ½ teaspoon thyme, ⅓ cup dry bread crumbs and 1 egg.

⇒PORK SECTION⇐

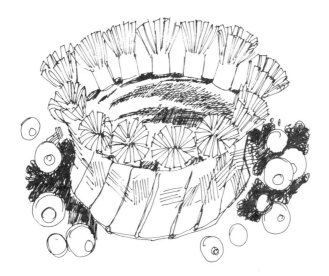

CROWN ROAST OF PORK

Serves 8 - 10

crown roast of pork
2 teaspoons salt
½ teaspoon black pepper
2 teaspoons Worcestershire sauce
1½ pounds prunes, pitted
2 cups water

3 cups peeled, sliced cooking apples
1 cup dry bread crumbs
¼ cup chopped green pepper
½ cup chopped celery
¼ cup melted butter or
    margarine

- Rub crown of pork with a mixture of salt, pepper and Worcestershire sauce.
- Place on foil covered rack in a roasting pan.

DRESSING

- Wash prunes, combine with water and apples, bring to boil.
- Remove from heat, let soak 5 minutes, drain well; mix with bread crumbs, green pepper, celery and butter; fill the center of the crown.
- Cover bone ends with foil or potato cubes; cover the filling with aluminum foil.
- Roast in a 325°F. oven 3½ hours or until the pork is tender.

CRUSTY ROAST OF PORK

- Select a fresh ham or shoulder or loin of pork with the skin on. (Fresh shoulders and hams are usually available).
- Score the skin with a sharp knife, cutting through to the fat beneath. (Do this either in parallel cuts about ⅛-inch apart, or in ¼-inch squares.)
- Put the pork in a cold oven; roast at 325°F. until the meat thermometer reads 175°F. and the skin blisters.

31

GLAZED BACK BACON   Serves 4

1 pound piece back bacon
8 canned apricots
  mashed with a bit of juice

1 teaspoon freshly grated lemon peel
2 tablespoons brandy
2½ tablespoons brown sugar

- Arrange bacon in a small casserole. Mix apricots with the grated lemon peel and brandy, coat the piece of bacon thickly.
- Sprinkle generously and as evenly as possible with the brown sugar.
- Roast in a 400°F. oven 30 minutes, adding a little wine or orange juice to the bottom of the casserole if it starts to cook dry.

GLAZED PORK TENDERLOIN   Serves 4

1½ pounds pork tenderloin
1 clove garlic, minced
1 onion, diced
1½ tablespoons butter or margarine

½ green pepper, cut in inch squares
2 tablespoons cornstarch
1½ cups pie cherries
1 tablespoon sugar

- Place tenderloin in a casserole, roast at 450°F. oven ten minutes, reduce heat to 350°F., roast 35 minutes.
- Sauté garlic and onions in butter, add green pepper.
- Mix cornstarch with some of the juice from the cherries, stir until smooth, add the sugar and cherries.
- Add thickened and sweetened cherries to garlic and green pepper mixture.
- Pour over pork tenderloin and roast 15 minutes more or until a meat thermometer inserted in the meat reaches an internal temperature of 175°F.

LOIN OF PORK — BRAISED WITH BEER   Serves 8

5 pound pork loin roast
2½ cups chopped onions
2 cups diced carrots
1½ cups beer

1½ teaspoon salt
¼ teaspoon pepper
1 bay leaf
5 whole cloves

- Brown pork well on all sides in a kettle or Dutch oven; remove from pan.
- Sauté onions and carrots in pork drippings until soft. Stir in beer, salt, pepper, bay leaf and whole cloves. Return pork to kettle, cover.
- Cook in 350°F. oven 2 hours, or until pork is tender when pierced with a fork. Place pork on platter, keep warm.
- Pour cooking liquid from kettle into a large bowl. Skim off fat; remove bay leaf.
- Place liquid and solids in container of electric blender and whirl at low speed until smooth (or press through sieve).
- Pour sauce into saucepan, heat to boiling, stir often.
- Generously spoon the sauce over the pork after it has been sliced.

MARINATED ROAST LEG OF PORK   Serves 6-10

10 pound leg of pork
 3 medium onions, chopped
 2 cloves garlic, crushed
 1 cup wine vinegar

½ bottle Worcestershire sauce
 1 cup catsup
 2 whole allspice
   salt and pepper

- Puncture leg of pork with fork.
- Combine remaining ingredients; pour over pork and marinate for 3 days, turning once or twice each day.
- Cook in 300°F. oven 30 minutes per pound.
- Baste with sweet red wine while cooking, if desired.

ROAST LOIN OF PORK WITH VEGETABLES   Serves 8

1 pork loin (10 rib)
6 green apples, peeled halfway
   down, cored
6 potatoes, peeled
6 large onions, peeled

salt, pepper
1 cup apple cider or juice
2 tablespoons butter or margarine
   blended with 2 tablespoons flour

- Roast loin of pork in 350°F. oven 2 hours.
- Place vegetables around roast, roast 1 hour longer.
- Remove from oven, place vegetables on a heated platter; let meat stand 20 minutes, then carve and place in the centre of the plate.
- Meanwhile, pour off fat in roasting pan and place pan over high heat.
- Add one cup boiling cider and the butter and flour mixture, blend. Mix with the pan glaze and dripping.
- Season to taste. Serve gravy with meat.

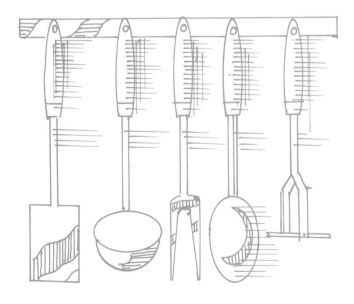

⊰LAMB SECTION⊱

LATIN STYLE SHOULDER OF LAMB
Serves 6

shoulder of lamb (about
  5 pounds) cut
2 cloves garlic, minced
1 teaspoon black pepper
12 anchovy fillets, finely minced
2 cloves
1 onion

1 bay leaf
3 sprigs parsley
½ cup beef broth
1 cup dry bread crumbs
½ teaspoon salt
½ teaspoon oregano
3 tablespoons cognac, optional

- Rub the lamb with a mixture of garlic, pepper and anchovy fillets; place in a shallow roasting pan.
- Stick the cloves in the onion and add to the pan with bay leaf, parsley and beef broth.
- Roast in a 450°F. oven 15 minutes, then cover the lamb with a mixture of the bread crumbs, salt and oregano.
- Reduce heat to 350°F. and continue roasting 15 to 20 minutes per pound, baste several times with the pan juices.
- Before serving, heat the cognac, set it aflame and pour over the lamb.
- Serve with gravy.

ROAST LEG OF LAMB
Serves 6 - 8

5 pound leg of lamb
1 tablespoon salt
1 teaspoon black pepper

2 cloves garlic, minced
1 teaspoon rosemary

- Rub the lamb with a mixture of salt, pepper, garlic and rosemary; let stand 1 hour.
- Place on a rack in a roasting pan; roast in a 350°F. oven 2½ hours or until meat is tender, baste frequently.
- Place on a hot serving dish; let stand 20 minutes before carving.

Variations:

FLORENTINE STYLE

- Make a marinade of ½ cup olive or salad oil and ⅓ cup wine vinegar; pour over seasoned lamb and marinate overnight; drain.
- Roast as above for 1 hour; mix marinade with 1 cup dry red wine; pour over roast and roast for 1½ hours longer, basting frequently.

34

EUROPEAN ROAST LEG OF LAMB   Serves 6

5-6 pound leg of lamb
2 cloves garlic, slivered
pepper
1½ tablespoons rosemary

2 tablespoons butter or margarine
⅓ cup olive oil
½ cup Marsala wine

- Insert garlic slivers here and there in leg of lamb, pushing in with a skewer as far as possible.
- Rub the lamb with pepper and the rosemary.
- Melt the butter and mix with olive oil and Wine to use as a basting liquid.
- Brown the lamb in the oven at 400°F. for 10 minutes, then reduce temperature to 325°F. and cook for 2 hours or until the meat is done as you prefer. 140°F. pink, 175°F. no pink.
- Baste from time to time with the basting liquid.

GREEK STYLE ROAST LAMB   Serves 6

1 five pound leg of lamb, trimmed
1 bunch green onions, chopped
1 lemon, chopped
1 small bunch fresh mint, chopped

1 teaspoon salt
¼ teaspoon freshly ground pepper
3 cups boiling water
4 tablespoons flour

- Place lamb, trimmed side up, on rack in shallow roasting pan.
- Blend onion, lemon, mint with ½ teaspoon salt and pepper.
- Press all but ¼ cup of mixture onto surface of lamb; pour 3 cups boiling water into pan.
- Roast in 425°F. oven 15 minutes; reduce heat to 325°F. and roast 2 hours and 15 minutes, basting several times with water in pan.
- Remove roast from pan to heated platter, sprinkle with reserved green onion mixture. Keep warm.
- Strain liquid in roasting pan into 4-cup measure; allow to stand 5 minutes; skim off all fat.
- Return liquid to roasting pan; heat to boiling.
- Combine flour with ½ cup cold water to make a smooth paste; stir into bubbling liquid.
- Cook, stirring constantly, until mixture thickens and bubbles 3 minutes. Season with remaining salt and serve in heated gravy boat.

ROAST SHOULDER OF LAMB   Serves 6

shoulder of lamb (about 5 pounds)
2½ teaspoons salt
¾ teaspoon black pepper

2 cloves garlic, minced
½ cup beef broth
½ cup dry red wine

- Rub lamb with a mixture of salt, pepper and garlic.
- Roast in a 400°F. oven 20 minutes; pour off the fat; add the broth and wine; roast 2 hours longer or to desired degree of doneness; basting frequently.

➣POULTRY SECTION ⬳

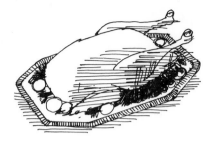

COUNTRY ROAST CHICKEN   Serves 8

2 3 pound broiler-fryers	1 onion, chopped
1 cup water	½ cup sliced celery
½ teaspoon salt	½ cup butter or margarine
1 8 ounce package bread-stuffing mix	¼ cup bacon drippings

- Remove giblets and necks from chicken packages and place (except livers) with water and salt in saucepan; cover.
- Simmer 45 minutes. Add livers; cover; simmer 15 minutes; cool.
- Remove giblets and necks from broth; reserve broth.
- Chop giblets and the meat from necks; place in a large bowl; stir in stuffing mix.
- Simmer reserved broth until reduced to ½ cup; reserve.
- Sauté onion and celery in the ½ cup butter or margarine for 5 minutes.
- Add with reserved broth to stuffing mixture; toss until evenly moistened.
- Stuff neck and body cavities lightly with stuffing. Skewer neck skin to back; close body cavity and tie legs to tail.
- Place chickens on rack in roasting pan. Brush with part of bacon drippings.
- Roast in 350°F. oven basting every 30 minutes with bacon drippings or butter, 1½ hours, or until tender.

RANCH STYLE CHICKEN   Serves 6

- Cut 3 frying chickens into pieces. Brush with melted butter or margarine, and place over coals for about 5 minutes to sear, and then turn.
- Brush with sauce and turn every 3 to 5 minutes, brushing with sauce at each turn. Time required is about 45 minutes.

Basting sauce:

½ cup apple cider or juice	2 teaspoons salt
⅓ cup salad oil	1 teaspoon paprika
1½ teaspoons Worcestershire	1½ teaspoons tomato paste
½ teaspoon minced onion	6 drops Tabasco
1 clove garlic, minced	¼ teaspoon dry mustard

- Best to make the sauce at least 24 hours before using.

ROAST TURKEY BREAST WITH OLIVE DRESSING   Serves 12

1 large onion, chopped
1 cup chopped celery
1 clove of garlic, crushed
6 tablespoons vegetable oil
3 cups cubed white bread (6 slices)
1 teaspoon salt
2 teaspoons leaf oregano, crumbled

½ teaspoon pepper
½ cup water
4 ounce jar small stuffed green olives, drained
1 turkey breast from 12 pound turkey (about 5 pounds)
turkey gravy

- Sauté onion, celery and garlic until soft in 3 tablespoons of the oil in a large frying pan.
- Add bread cubes, ½ teaspoon of the salt, 1 teaspoon of the oregano, ¼ teaspoon of the pepper, water and olives; toss to blend well.
- Spoon bread dressing in a mound on bottom of a shallow roasting pan.
- Place turkey breast over stuffing.
- Combine remaining 3 tablespoons oil, remaining salt, remaining oregano and ¼ teaspoon of the pepper in cup. Brush over turkey breast to coat well.
- Roast in 375°F. oven (2 hours) basting often with pan drippings or until turkey is tender and a deep golden brown. Transfer breast and stuffing to heated serving platter; keep warm while making gravy.

ROAST TURKEY
WITH SWEET AND SOUR SAUCE   Serves 10

1 large onion, chopped
5 tablespoons butter or margarine
2 cups rice
3 cups rich chicken or beef stock

½ pound cooked ham, diced
salt, pepper
10-12 pound turkey

- Sauté the onion in butter; add rice and mix well; add stock and simmer slowly until all the stock is absorbed but the rice is slightly undercooked.
- Add ham, salt and pepper; stuff the turkey with this mixture; cover with a tent of foil; cook in a 325°F. oven for approximately 3 hours or until the drumsticks move easily and the juices run clear when skin is punctured at the joint; remove the foil for the last 30 minutes to allow the turkey to brown.

SWEET AND SOUR SAUCE

2 slices pineapple, chopped
1 teaspoon chopped preserved ginger (optional)
oil for frying
6 tablespoons chopped onion
1 tablespoon vinegar

1 tablespoon tomato catsup
1 tablespoon soya sauce
1 teaspoon sherry
1 teaspoon cornstarch mixed with 1½ cups water

- Fry pineapple and ginger in oil for a few minutes.
- Add onion and fry until tender; add other ingredients; simmer slowly 5 - 10 minutes; serve with turkey.

❧VARIETY MEAT SECTION❧

BAKED TONGUE   Serves 6 - 8

5-pound fresh beef tongue
1½ cups sliced onions
1 teaspoon salt
½ teaspoon black pepper
½ teaspoon basil

2 cloves garlic, minced
1 bay leaf
2 cups canned tomatoes
2 cups boiling water

- Cover tongue with boiling water and cook 10 minutes; drain, cool, remove skin and root.
- Place in roasting pan with onions; sprinkle with salt, pepper, basil and garlic; add bay leaf, tomatoes and water.
- Cover pan and bake in a 325°F. oven 3 hours or until tender.
- Baste frequently and remove the cover for the last 30 minutes.

POT-ROASTS FAMILY STYLE

Pot Roast is a term applied to larger cuts of meat which are cooked by braising in a small amount of liquid or in steam. The meat may or may not be browned in a little fat before it is braised.

Lean or less tender cuts of meat, those which would be too dry or too tough if roasted, are generally used for pot roasts, although any meat or poultry, including tender cuts, can be used.

The beef cuts most suitable for pot roasts are: blade, arm, boneless shoulder or chuck, rolled boned rump, eye of the round, heel of the round, boned and rolled sirloin tip, brisket and flank.

Lamb is such a tender meat that all its cuts may be roasted. However, for pot-roasting these cuts can be used: shoulder, breast and rolled breast.

Like lamb, pork cuts are so tender that they are usually roasted. However, any of these cuts can be pot-roasted: Boston butt, rolled Boston butt, fresh picnic, loin and leg (fresh ham).

The veal cuts best for pot roasts are: blade, breast, rolled shoulder and boned and rolled rump.

Among the variety meats whole livers, kidneys and hearts can be pot-roasted.

Whole chickens, ducklings and small turkeys can be pot-roasted.

Pot-roasting is similar to braising but uses a little more liquid to create steam. The amount of liquid used will depend on the tenderness of the cut and whether vegetables are to be added during cooking.

First, prepare meat for pot-roasting according to recipe instructions and follow method for each recipe.

 BEEF SECTION

PLAIN POT ROAST   Serves 4 - 6

- Choose a piece of beef weighing 4 to 6 pounds.
- Dredge the meat with flour, pepper and salt.
- Melt 4 tablespoons butter or margarine in a deep pot and brown meat on all sides.
- Add ½ to 1 cup liquid. (This may be water, stock, wine or tomato juice.)
- Reduce the heat, cover tightly and simmer slowly for 25 minutes per pound or until meat is tender.
- The meat should be tender enough to cut easily but not stringy and mushy; if the liquid evaporates, add more.

Variations   BARBECUED POT ROAST

- Add 1½ cups sliced onions and 1 clove garlic, minced, to browned meat and cook until browned.
- Mix in

1 teaspoon salt   8 ounce can tomato sauce
½ teaspoon pepper

- Cover and cook over low heat 1½ hours.
- Stir in

¼ cup chili sauce   2 teaspoons Worcestershire sauce
⅓ cup cider vinegar   ½ cup water
2 tablespoons brown sugar   2 teaspoons chili powder

- Cover and cook 1 hour longer or until tender.

Variations (continued)

SPICED BEEF POT ROAST

- Add to browned meat and liquid 2 tablespoons mixed pickling spice; simmer covered for 2 - 2½ hours.
- Add 2 teaspoons salt and 1 pound mixed dried fruits; simmer 1 hour longer.

    To serve: Slice meat, pour liquid over top, garnish with fruit; serve with hot cooked noodles.

MARINATED POT ROAST

- Soak 4 pound pot roast of beef in marinade for 12 - 24 hours; drain, dry, brown on all sides in heavy pan.
- Add marinade, cover and simmer for 3 hours.
- Serve with gravy.

MARINADES
Apple Cider

1 onion, sliced	small piece of stick cinnamon
6 whole cloves	1 teaspoon salt
piece of ginger root	2 cups apple cider

German Style Marinade

2 cups cider vinegar	2 bay leaves
1 cup water	2 teaspoons salt
8 peppercorns	2 cloves garlic, minced
3 cloves	1 cup sliced onion

- Simmer pot roast in marinade **and**

1½ cups chopped onion	2 tablespoons sugar
1 cup grated carrots	

- Add 1 cup sour cream to gravy.

NEW ENGLAND-STYLE BOILED DINNER   Serves 4

3 pounds corned beef brisket	5 or 6 small carrots
1 medium onion	5 or 6 small onions
1 bay leaf	4 whole beets, cooked, skinned
1 garlic clove	1 tablespoon caraway seeds
5 peppercorns	1 head cabbage, coarsely shredded
4 potatoes	

- Wash corned beef; put in kettle and cover with boiling water.
- Add next 4 ingredients; cover and simmer for 3½ hours or until meat is tender.
- Add potatoes, carrots and small onions to meat during last 35 minutes of cooking.
- Add caraway seeds and small amount of broth to cabbage; cook for 10 to 12 minutes, or until tender.
- Put cabbage on centre of platter, cover with sliced meat and arrange other vegetables around.

BOILED BEEF SUPPER

Serves 6

3-4 lbs bottom round beef,
tied for a pot roast
6 carrots, peeled and cut in
2 inch pieces

⅓ cup finely chopped parsley
3 leeks, split, quartered, washed,
and cut in 2 inch pieces
salt and pepper

- Sear the beef on both sides in a Dutch oven.
- Add carrots, parsley, leeks, and water almost to cover the meat.
- Cover and simmer 2-3 hours over low heat.
- Season in the last 5 minutes before serving.
- Serve the broth separately, and the beef sliced on a platter surrounded by the vegetables.

POT-ROASTED FLANK STEAK WITH VEGETABLES

Serves 4

1 flank steak (about 2 pounds)
½ cup chopped celery tops
1 onion, chopped
few parsley sprigs, chopped
½ teaspoon thyme
2 teaspoons salt

½ teaspoon pepper
1 tablespoon shortening
1 cup water
8 small whole carrots
8 small potatoes

- Pound steak with rolling pin or mallet until both sides are slightly flattened.
- Sprinkle with celery tops, onion, parsley, thyme, half of salt and the pepper.
- Roll up jelly-roll fashion, beginning at the pointed end; tie with string.
- Brown on all sides in hot shortening; add water; simmer, covered, for 1½ hours, turning meat occasionally, and adding more water if necessary.
- Add vegetables and remaining salt and pepper; simmer for 30 minutes longer.
- To serve, slice meat diagonally.

CHUCK ROAST TERIYAKI

Serves 8

7 to 8 pounds chuck roast,
about 2 inches thick

Meat tenderizer

Teriyaki Sauce

1 cup soy sauce
¼ cup sherry
1 tablespoon powdered ginger

2 cloves garlic
1 teaspoon sugar

- Cut all bone and fat from meat (use for a soup stock), cut up lean pieces.
- Sprinkle meat liberally with tenderizer, let stand — (follow the manufacturer's directions.) Marinate about 1 hour in teriyaki sauce.
- Broil meat slowly over a charcoal fire for about 1½ hours, turning only once during the cooking.

⋙ VEAL SECTION ⋘

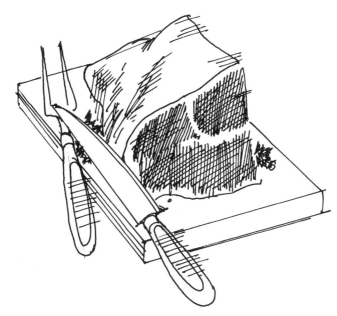

SPICY VEAL POT ROAST   Serves 8

5 pounds rump of veal
1 tablespoon each of brown sugar,
  powdered mustard and salt
½ teaspoon pepper
2 tablespoons cooking oil

2 tablespoons vinegar
1 teaspoon basil
1 clove garlic, minced
½ cup water

- Rub veal with mixture of sugar, mustard, salt and pepper; brown on all sides in oil; put meat on rack; add remaining ingredients.
- Simmer, covered, for 2½ hours or until meat is tender, basting occasionally with liquid in kettle, add more water if necessary.

VEAL POT ROAST ORIENTAL   Serves 4

¼ cup soy sauce
1 tablespoon vinegar
½ teaspoon each of salt and pepper
1 teaspoon ground ginger
2 pounds veal front

¼ cup all-purpose flour
3 tablespoons shortening
¾ cup boiling water
1 cup white onions, drained

- Mix soy sauce, vinegar and seasonings; pour over veal and let stand for at least 30 minutes, turning meat several times.
- Lift meat from marinade; roll in flour; brown in hot shortening; place on rack in kettle.
- Add marinade and boiling water; simmer, covered for 2 hours or until veal is tender.
- Add onions and heat.

43

⋙ PORK SECTION ⋘

SPICED PORK POT ROAST
Serves 8

1 fresh ham (about 5 pounds)
1½ cups water
1 teaspoon each of salt, thyme,
 sage and whole cloves
1½ teaspoons whole allspice

1 bay leaf, crumbled
1 tablespoon slivered lemon rind
2 tablespoons fresh lemon juice
1 medium onion, chopped
1 large carrot, diced

- Brown meat on all sides; pour off fat.
- Place meat on rack; put in kettle; add remaining ingredients; simmer, covered, for 4 hours or until meat is tender, basting occasionally with liquid in kettle.
- Add more water if necessary.
- Thicken liquid if desired.

FRESH PORK PICNIC POT ROAST
WITH VEGETABLES
Serves 4

3 pounds rolled fresh picnic
 shoulder
 all-purpose flour
 salt, pepper and paprika
2 tablespoons fat
2 cups water

1 bay leaf
1 clove garlic
4 sweet potatoes
4 large white turnips
½ medium head cabbage,
 cut into fourths

- Rub meat with flour, salt, pepper and paprika; brown on all sides in hot fat.
- Add water, bay leaf and garlic; bring to boil, cover and simmer for 1½ hours.
- Add potatoes and turnips cut into quarters; cook for 15 minutes.
- Add cabbage, cook for 20 minutes.
- Arrange meat and vegetables on hot platter.

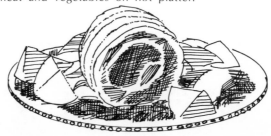

POT-ROASTED FRESH BOSTON BUTT
WITH VEGETABLES   Serves 4

1 fresh rolled Boston butt
  (about 2 pounds)
  salt and pepper
2 tablespoons fat
2 cups water

1 onion, sliced
8 small carrots
2½ cups potato cubes
2 cups fresh or frozen lima beans
4 ears corn

- Rub meat with salt and pepper; brown on all sides in hot fat.
- Add water and onion; bring to a boil; simmer, covered, for 2 hours or until meat is almost tender.
- Add carrots, potatoes and lima beans; cover, simmer for 20 minutes.
- Put corn on top, cover, cook for 10 minutes or until tender.
- Serve meat surrounded with vegetables.

LAMB SECTION

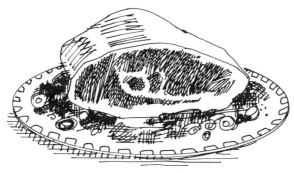

POT-ROASTED SHOULDER OF LAMB
WITH DILL SAUCE   Serves 4

3 pounds shoulder of lamb, cut
1 cup water
1 teaspoon dill seed

1 teaspoon salt
4 peppercorns
dill sauce

- Put lamb in kettle with all ingredients except dill sauce; simmer, covered for 2 hours or until meat is tender, adding more water if necessary.
- Remove meat; strain liquid.
- Pour dill sauce over meat.

DILL SAUCE

- Melt 2 tablespoons butter or margarine and blend in 2 tablespoons flour. Add 1¼ cups strained liquid, 1 teaspoon sugar and 1 teaspoon vinegar. Cook until thickened. Beat 1 egg yolk; stir in small amount of sauce; add to remainder of sauce and mix well. Season to taste.

LAMB SHANKS BARBECUED Serves 4

4 meaty lamb shanks
⅓ cup half brandy, half sherry
⅓ cup soy sauce

½ cup honey
2 tablespoons olive oil

- Heat brandy, sherry, soy sauce, and honey together briefly just enough to blend.
- Marinate the lamb shanks for 3-4 hours.
- Remove shanks from marinade, brown in oil in a frying pan.
- Transfer to a baking dish, add the marinade; cover and cook in a 350°F. oven 1½ hours, baste from time to time with marinade.

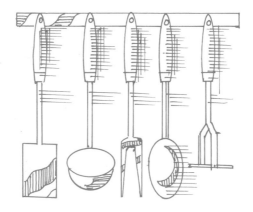

PUDDING STYLE YORKSHIRE CHICKEN Serves 6

3 pound broiler-fryer
3 tablespoons flour
   (for coating)
½ teaspoon salt
¼ teaspoon pepper
3 tablespoons vegetable oil
4 eggs

1½ cups milk
1½ cups sifted all-purpose flour
1 teaspoon paprika
¾ teaspoon salt
¼ teaspoon pepper
3 tablespoons butter or margarine, melted

- Cut chicken into serving size pieces. Combine the next 3 ingredients for coating in a plastic bag. Shake chicken pieces in bag to coat evenly.
- Brown chicken pieces well on all sides in oil in a large frying pan.
- Beat eggs until light in a medium size bowl; stir in milk. Sift flour, paprika, salt and pepper for batter over bowl.
- Beat only until batter is smooth. Stir in melted butter.
- Place a 2½ quart shallow baking dish in oven to heat while preheating the oven to 375°F.
- Pour batter into heated baking dish. Arrange chicken pieces in dish.
- Bake 45 minutes, or until golden and puffy.

BRAISED TURKEY

Serves 8-10

1 14 pound ready-to-cook turkey
  (fresh or frozen), thawed
½ cup butter or margarine
1 teaspoon salt
½ teaspoon pepper
12 sprigs parsley

2 cloves garlic
1 large onion, chopped
2 large carrots, chopped
2 stalks celery, chopped
2 cans condensed chicken broth
  flour

- Rinse turkey, dry thoroughly, cook giblets as desired.
- Place 3 tablespoons of the butter inside turkey cavity, then sprinkle cavity with ½ teaspoon salt and ¼ teaspoon of the pepper; fill with parsley.
- Tie legs in place; fasten wings to side with skewers.
- Tie string around middle of bird to make turning easier.
- Sprinkle outside of turkey with remaining salt and pepper.
- Place turkey in a deep large roasting pan with a tight fitting cover; add remaining 5 tablespoons butter to pan.
- Brown in 425°F. oven 15 minutes; brush turkey with melted butter; turn turkey one quarter; stir in chopped onion, carrot and celery.
- Continue roasting and turning turkey until brown, about 1 hour.
- Turn turkey, breast-side-down in roasting pan; pour chicken broth over; cover turkey with a double thickness of foil; cover pan.
- Braise in 350°F. oven 2 hours, or until juices run clear yellow when thigh meat is pierced with a fork.
- Remove turkey to heated platter; cut off strings; keep warm.
- Strain liquid into a bowl; allow to cool until all fat has floated to the top; skim off all fat. Pour liquid into a medium-size saucepan; add flour, smoothed to a paste with a little of cold water.
- Heat to boiling, lower heat, stirring constantly, until sauce thickens slightly. Season to taste.

VARIETY MEAT SECTION

BEEF HEART SAUTEED

Serves 5

2-3 beef hearts, sliced
  (depending on size)
3 tablespoons bacon fat or a mixture
  of butter and oil

⅓ cup red wine
1½ tablespoons finely chopped parsley
  salt and pepper

- Sauté the heart in fat until almost tender; add wine, parsley, salt and pepper.
- Simmer a few minutes more. (Cooking time should be 15-20 minutes).

CALVES HEARTS, DRESSED WITH APRICOT AND ONION

Serves 5

2 calves' hearts (tubes, fat membrane, and fat cut out)
⅓ cup chopped dried apricots
1 onion, chopped

1 teaspoon rosemary
2 tablespoon butter or margarine
1 cup bouillon plus juice of half lemon
salt and pepper

- Stuff hearts with a mixture of the apricots, onion, and rosemary.
- Sauté briefly in half of the butter and transfer to a small casserole that fits rather snugly.
- Dot tops of hearts with the rest of the butter, pour wine into the casserole.
- Roast in a 350°F. oven about an hour and a half or until the hearts are tender, basting occasionally with the juices in the casserole.

SAVOURY TRIPE

Serves 5

1½ pounds cooked tripe
2 cups strained cooking liquid
1 tablespoon chopped parsley
¼ teaspoon thyme
½ teaspoon marjoram
¼ teaspoon ground ginger
2 whole cloves

⅛ teaspoon pepper
dash cayenne pepper
1 cup diced carrots
½ cup sliced onion
2 to 2½ tablespoons flour
1 teaspoon vinegar

- Brown tripe in fat; add cooking liquid, seasonings, carrots and sliced onion, cover, simmer 30 minutes.
- To thicken, mix flour to a smooth paste with 3 to 4 tablespoons cold water; blend with some of the hot cooking liquid; stir gradually into tripe mixture and cook until smooth and thickened, about 5 minutes; add vinegar.

STEAKS, CHOPS AND BARBECUE MEALS

BROILING AND FRYING

How to Broil

Broiling is a dry heat method of cooking thin tender cuts. Directions vary with type of broiler unit used, thickness and kind of meat and degree of doneness desired.

— Preheat broiler. Leave door ajar.

— Snip fat edge of meat to prevent curling.

— Place meat on cold rack of broiler pan at recommended distance from heat.

— Broil meat on both sides to desired stage of doneness.

— Season meat as each side is browned.

Steaks and chops should be cut at least 1-inch thick for broiling; slices of ham should be at least ½-inch thick. The top surface of 1-inch steaks or chops should be 2 to 3 inches from the heat; 2-inch cuts, 3 to 5 inches from heat. Reduce temperature if distance must be less. (One turning is all that's necessary.)

To Broil Frozen Steak

Preheat broiler, then broil unthawed meat 3 or 4 inches from heat, depending on thickness. Allow longer total cooking time than for similar cuts at room temperature.

Pan-broiling

Preheat a heavy frying pan. Rub with some meat fat to prevent sticking. Brown meat on both sides. Season.

Reduce temperature and finish cooking. Do not cover. Do not add water. Pour off fat as it accumulates in the pan. Turn occasionally to cook meat evenly.

How to Panfry

Panfrying is a dry heat method of cooking thin, tender cuts.
— Use a heavy frying pan.
— Add a small amount of fat or fat cut from the meat.
— Snip fat edge of meat to prevent curling.
— Brown meat on both sides.
— Season meat after browning.
— Avoid pricking meat to prevent juices escaping—use tongs to turn meat.
— Do not cover pan except as directed for certain meats.
— Cook to desired stage of doneness.
— Serve with gravy.
— When cooking fat meat do not add fat. Cook in ungreased pan, uncovered and pour off excess fat. This is sometimes called "pan-broiling".

Braising

Small cuts of less tender meat and many tender types as well are excellent braised. For braising choose a shallow heavy pan or frying pan with a close-fitting cover to prevent steam from escaping during cooking. The initial preparation of meat for braising may include:

1. Marinating in a spicy mixture containing some acid—vinegar, lemon juice or wine—that acts as a tenderizer; adds flavour and provides moisture.
2. Pounding to break down coarse grain of meat, a step sometimes suggested for round steak.
3. Scoring in crisscross pattern with a sharp knife opens up the meat surface at intervals and helps to shorten the cooking time.
   During pounding, scoring or cubing, meat may be dredged or dusted with seasoned or plain flour depending on the recipe. Follow recipe instructions for cooking.

⇒BARBECUES⇐

Barbecues—the word has a different meaning—for many people. It covers food cooked over an open fire, over coals, in a pit, on a spit, in front of a fire.

You can have barbecues with whole animals, poultry, fish or small cuts. It can mean a party out-of-doors.

Meats to be barbecued are tastier and more moist if marinated before or brushed with a sauce during cooking.

Barbecues are fun for the whole family and the food always tastes better.

Barbecuing or Oven-spit Roasting

In ancient times the haunch of venison, the wild boar and rows of pheasants were cooked to savoury perfection on a constantly revolving spit over the dancing flames of an open fireplace. This dry-heat method of cooking has had an exciting revival with the introduction of motorized spits.

Set spit in rotiserrie position and place a shallow pan on rack below meat to catch drips, adding just enough hot water to cover the bottom. Replace water as it evaporates.

As with oven-roasting, a meat thermometer is the surest way of knowing the internal temperature, whether inserted at the start of cooking or further along. Insert the thermometer into the thickest part of the lean meat being careful that the point is not resting on a bone, in fat or on the spit.

Any tender cuts of meat that you ordinarily roast such as rolled or standing ribs of beef, ham or leg of lamb, turkey and spareribs, can be spit-roasted on a rotisserie or at a barbecue.

You can thread on a skewer any food that cooks in a reasonable length of time. Remember, however, that you can't mix short-cooking and long-cooking foods on the same spit.

To baste a large assortment of foods you will need three different sauces:

Sauce No. 1: Soy, wine and oil seasoned with mashed garlic.

Sauce No. 2: Tomato-base barbecue sauce.

Sauce No. 3: Lemon-butter seasoned with herbs.

HERE ARE A FEW KABOB COMBINATIONS:

1. Round steak with small green onions. Weave strips of meat around onion bulbs on skewer, working close to the point of skewer. Grill. (Sauce No. 1.)

Barbecues (continued)

2. Bacon-pineapple roll-ups; sweet pickle chunks. Grill slowly until bacon is done. Drippings provide natural basting sauce. Bacon keeps pineapple from falling off skewer.
3. Green pepper strips; whole small white boiling onions (or canned onions); bacon; round steak strips. Roll up thin round steak strips loosely so meat cooks in centre. Bacon supplies some fat. Grill slowly. (Sauce No. 1 or No. 2.)
4. Orange sections; ham and olive roll-ups. Ham supplies some fat so light basting of oil is sufficient.
5. Onion quarters; marinated lamb; green pepper; tomato. Add additional oil or butter to marinade for sauce.
6. Apple and ham. Butter or oil provides necessary fat; last-minute brushing with honey glazes meat, fruit.
7. Mushrooms; bacon; chicken livers. Weave bacon around chicken livers. Grill slowly. (Sauce No. 1 or No. 3.)
8. Ripe olives; prawns; pimiento. Food is cooked so needs only browning. (Sauce No. 3.)
9. Potato; chunks of wieners; canned artichoke hearts. Use cooked small potatoes or canned potatoes. Skewer artichokes through the hearts. Needs only heating, browning. (Sauce No. 3 plus some prepared mustard.)

⇒ BARBECUES ⇐

BARBECUED STEAK   Serves 4

¼ cup butter or margarine
1 clove garlic, chopped fine
¾ teaspoon salt
  paprika

¼ teaspoon Worcestershire sauce
  top sirloin steak, 1½ inches
  thick
6 or 8 rolls

- Melt butter, mash garlic and salt together; add to butter with paprika and Worcestershire.
- As mixture boils, brush the upper side of the steak.
- Turn the steak about four times during the cooking; and brush each time with the butter mixture.
- While the steak is cooking, slice 6 or 8 wiener rolls in half.
- Brush with the remaining sauce and toast over the coals.

MARINADE FOR STEAK

⅔ cup salad oil
½ teaspoon fresh ground pepper
  dash of salt

juice of 1 lemon
1 clove garlic

- Mix first four ingredients, rub the meat lightly with a clove of garlic before placing it in the oil.
- Let steak stand in this marinade in a cool place 12 or 15 hours, turn it several times.
- When ready to broil, remove the steak from the oil and grill as usual.

MARINATED STEAK VARIATIONS

PAN-BROILED OR SAUTEED:

Using a heavy frying pan, melt 2 tablespoons butter or fat from the steak. Increase heat, place steak in very hot pan, and sear quickly on one side. Reduce the heat a little and allow a 1½ inch steak to cook 8 to 9 minutes before turning. Salt and pepper, turn, brown well on the other side and cook until done. Serve with butter and the sauce from the pan.

BARBECUED:

Brush steak well with 1 teaspoon salt, 2 teaspoons dry mustard and enough water to make a thick paste. Allow to stand ½ hour before broiling.

MINUTE:

Minute steaks are cut from the loin or the sirloin and may be anywhere from 3/16 to ½ inch thick. They should be pan-broiled or sautéed very quickly and served at once. If you like them rare, merely a quick searing on each side will be sufficient.

MINUTE, SOUTH AMERICAN:

This is an ideal dish to cook at the table.

Melt ½ cup butter in a large, heavy-bottomed frying pan. Add the steaks, sear them very quickly on both sides and place them on a very hot platter. To the pan add 2 tablespoons chopped green onion, 1 teaspoon salt, ½ teaspoon coarse black pepper, 2 tablespoons finely chopped parsley and 2 tablespoons steak sauce. Allow to cook together for 2 minutes. Add 6 tablespoons red wine, let the sauce heat through thoroughly, pour at once over the steaks.

BEDEVILED BEEF SLICES   Serves 4

8 slices cooked beef
  (¼ inch thick)
3 tablespoons prepared mustard
1 egg
½ teaspoon salt

4 drops tabasco sauce
2 tablespoons water
1 cup seasoned fine dry bread
  crumbs
3 tablespoons vegetable oil

- Spread beef slices with the prepared mustard.
- Beat egg; stir in salt and water.
- Sprinkle bread crumbs on wax paper.
- Dip beef slices first into seasoned egg and then bread crumbs.
- Heat oil in a large frying pan; brown beef slices on one side; turn and brown on second side. Serve on a heated platter.

BROILED FLANK STEAK   Serves 4

1 flank steak, 2-3 pounds, cut
  against grain in 1½ inch wide
  strips
  large mushroom caps (at least
  2 apiece)

  butter or margarine
4 tomatoes, halved
  mayonnaise
  finely chopped onion
  salt and pepper

- Wipe off mushroom caps with a piece of lemon. Remove stems, save.
- Put ½ teaspoon butter in each cap.
- Mix mayonnaise with onion and pile lossely on each cut tomato half.
- Place flank steak about 3 inches from the broiler. After 2-3 minutes, add the tomato halves, placing them at the side.
- After 5 minutes on one side for rare, turn and add the mushrooms.
- Remove when done, and serve immediately.

BUTTERFLY STEAK

Serves 4 - 6

2 tablespoons olive oil
1 tablespoon butter or margarine
1/8 teaspoon sage
1/4 teaspoon rosemary
1/2 teaspoon finely crushed bay leaf

1 1/2 pounds filet of beef, split length-
    wise and pounded lightly
3/4 teaspoon salt
1/4 teaspoon black pepper
3 tablespoons warm cognac, optional

- Heat the oil and butter in frying pan; add sage, rosemary and bay leaf, then meat.
- Cook over high heat 2 minutes on each side or to desired degree of doneness.
- Season with salt and pepper; pour the cognac over and set aflame.
- Turn filet over for a few seconds, then serve.

CHINESE-STYLE PEPPER STEAK

Serves 6 - 8

3 pounds sirloin of beef
1 tablespoon cornstarch
1/4 cup water
3 cloves garlic, minced
1 teaspoon ginger
3/4 cup peanut or vegetable oil
1 1/2 cups chopped onions

2 green peppers, cut julienne
2 tomatoes, cut in small wedges
1 teaspoon sugar
1 teaspoon salt
1/4 teaspoon black pepper
1 cup chicken broth
4 tablespoons dry sherry

- Cut the meat into thin strips, 2 inches long.
- Mix cornstarch with water until smooth; add garlic, ginger and beef.
- Heat oil in a frying pan; cook the meat mixture over high heat 5 minutes, stirring constantly; remove.
- Add onions, green peppers and tomatoes; cook over medium heat, stirring frequently, 2 minutes; stir in sugar, salt, pepper, broth and sherry; cook 3 minutes.
- Add meat and cook 2 minutes longer, stirring; serve immediately with boiled rice.

CRUMBED CHUCK BROIL
Serves 6

2 pound bone-in chuck steak
⅔ cup wine vinegar
2 tablespoons vegetable oil
1 onion, chopped
2 tablespoons prepared mustard

½ teaspoon pepper
2 cups soft white bread crumbs
2 tablespoons melted butter
or margarine

- Trim excess fat from steak and score remaining fat edge every inch. Place steak in a shallow dish.
- Mix vinegar, oil, onion, mustard and pepper in a bowl; pour over steak. Marinate in refrigerator, turning once, (at least 2 hours).
- Remove steak from marinade, pat dry.
- Rub broiler rack with oil. Broil steak 4 inches from heat, 5 minutes; turn steak; broil 5 minutes longer, or until it is cooked as you prefer.
- Remove broiler pan from heat; top steak evenly with prepared crumbs.
- Return steak to broiler and broil 2 minutes longer, or until crumbs are golden.
- Remove to serving platter; slice and serve.

DOUBLE PEPPER BEEF
Serves 6

2 medium size green peppers, halved,
  seeded and thinly sliced
2 medium size sweet red peppers,
  halved, seeded and thinly sliced
2 tablespoons vegetable oil
1½ pounds boneless chuck steak

1 cup water
1½ teaspoon Italian seasoning,
  crumbled
¾ teaspoon salt
½ teaspoon pepper

- Sauté peppers in oil until soft; remove to hot platter; keep warm.
- Cook steak in oil remaining in frying pan turning once, 5 minutes on each side or until steak is cooked as you like it. Slice steak, across grain and arrange with peppers on hot platter.
- Stir water, Italian seasoning, salt and pepper into pan. Cook, stirring constantly, scraping to loosen cooked-on juices in skillet.
- Boil 3 minutes to reduce volume by one-third. Pour over sliced beef and peppers. Serve with hot cooked rice.

EASTERN BARBECUED BEEF

Serves 6

3 pounds lean beef (chuck,
   sirloin tips, or steak)
¾ cup salad oil
¼ cup sugar
2 tablespoons soy sauce
4 tablespoons finely chopped
   green onion

2 cloves garlic, minced
½ teaspoon salt
½ teaspoon pepper
4 tablespoons sesame seed

- Cut beef in rather thin slices or strips. Mix remaining ingredients and pour over meat. Be sure that meat is well covered with sauce. Let stand overnight in refrigerator.

- Remove from refrigerator and bring to room temperature. When ready to broil over hot coals, drain off extra sauce. Cook on narrow-mesh grill or thread on skewers. Baste with sauce as necessary during broiling.

EASY PEPPER STEAK

Serves 4

4 rib steaks, trimmed of fat
2 tablespoons coarsely cracked
   black pepper

⅓ cup butter
2 tablespoons olive oil
2 tablespoons brandy

- Press the peppercorns with your hand liberally on either side of the steaks.

- Wrap loosely in paper and let stand 3 hours or overnight, so flavor permeates the steak.

- Broil. Make a sauce of the rest of the ingredients and pour over the steak when serving.

MARINATED BROILED STEAK

   sirloin, porterhouse or individual
   wing steaks, cut 1 inch thick
½ cup olive oil
¼ cup lemon juice
1 teaspoon salt

½ teaspoon black pepper
1 clove garlic, minced
1 tablespoon minced parsley
2 tablespoons butter

- Mix oil, lemon juice, salt, pepper, garlic and parsley.

- Marinate steak in the mixture for several hours at room temperature, turning frequently, drain.

- Barbecue to desired degree of doneness; spread butter over the steak.

- Serve with foil-baked potatoes and a caesar-style salad.

MORNING STYLE STEAK

1 steak, medium thick
1 tablespoon olive oil
  dash salt
  dash onion powder

dash garlic powder
dash pepper, freshly ground
bay leaves

- Brush the steak on both sides with olive oil. Sprinkle liberally with seasonings, place on the grill, and cook as desired. Before removing the meat, quickly burn a spray of bay leaves under one side and then the other.

ORIENTAL BARBECUED FILET MIGNON   Serves 4

1 pound filet of beef, sliced
  and pounded thin
4 tablespoons soya sauce
2 tablespoons dry sherry
1 teaspoon powdered ginger
1 teaspoon sugar

⅛ teaspoon black pepper
½ cup vegetable oil
2 pounds spinach, washed, drained
  and shredded
1 teaspoon salt

- Marinate the beef for 2 hours in next 5 ingredients.
- Heat 3 tablespoons oil in frying pan and fry the spinach 3 minutes, stirring frequently; stir in salt.
- Heat remaining oil; sauté the beef over high heat 2 minutes, turning the slices once.
- Arrange spinach on a hot serving dish; place beef on top and pour juices from sautéed beef over all.

OVEN-GRILLED CHEESE STEAK   Serves 6

3½ pound chuck steak
¼ cup bottled steak sauce

¼ cup chopped pecans
½ cup grated Cheddar cheese

- Brush both sides with steak sauce and leave at room temperature for 1 hour; place on rack in broiler pan placed close to the heat source.
- Heat in 450°F. oven 25 minutes for rare, or until done as you like steak; remove from oven; turn off heat.
- Sprinkle pecans, then cheese over steak; return to heated oven just until cheese melts.
- Carve into ¼ inch thick slices; across grain spoon juices over.

SAUCES AND MARINADES

There is no mystery about the composition of barbecue sauces and marinades. They are a blend of three main ingredients: oil, seasonings and a food acid such as lemon juice, vinegar, wine or tomato juice. They are used to sharpen the flavour of meats, fowl or fish and to supply fat to meats that are lacking in natural oils. Some cooks believe that the food acids help to tenderize the meat.

Meats are soaked in marinades to flavour and sometimes to tenderize them before they are put on the grill or spit. Some durable cuts profit from prolonged marinating—two or three days; most need only to be left for a few hours in the flavourful bath. Usually the marinade may also be used as a basting sauce.

Some are served as is; some can be mixed with drippings to make gravy.

BARBECUE SAUCE (I)

1 cup tomato juice
1 cup consomme
1 tablespoon meat sauce
  tarragon
  thyme
  cloves
1 tablespoon freshly ground pepper

1 tablespoon salt
2 tablespoons wine vinegar
2 tablespoons onion juice
1 tablespoon brown sugar
1 clove garlic, grated
½ cup sherry
  parsley

- Heat tomato juice, consomme and meat sauce with a sprig of tarragon, a sprig of thyme and 2 or 3 whole cloves.
- Just before boiling, add other seasonings; add sherry and allow it to heat for a minute or two longer before it is served.

BARBECUE SAUCE (II)

2 cloves garlic
½ cup olive oil
2 tablespoons anchovy paste
2 cups consomme

2 tablespoons meat sauce
  salt
¼ teaspoon cayenne pepper
1 tablespoon minute tapioca

- Sauté garlic cloves in oil; add anchovy paste, mix thoroughly; add consomme, meat sauce and other seasonings.
- Simmer about 5 minutes; add tapioca for thickening.
- Allow mixture to boil up and when it begins to thicken, remove from fire.

BARBECUE SAUCE (III)

½ pound bacon, diced
¼ cup chopped onion
2 garlic cloves, chopped
¼ cup chopped celery
tarragon
rosemary
thyme
1 tablespoon salt

1 teaspoon pepper
cayenne pepper
ground cloves
2 pounds fresh tomatoes, quartered
2 cups consomme
1 tablespoon sugar
1 green pepper, chopped
parsley

- Sauté bacon, add onion, garlic, celery, a sprig of tarragon, a pinch of rosemary and a pinch of thyme; add salt, pepper and a generous dash of cayenne and a pinch of ground cloves.
- Cook together 4 or 5 minutes; add tomatoes, consomme and sugar; simmer about 40 minutes or until smooth and velvety.
- Add finely chopped green pepper and about 3 tablespoons chopped parsley; cook about 5 minutes longer.

SAUTEED BEEF FILETS AND ONIONS   Serves 6

6 filets of beef, cut ½ inch thick
6 tablespoons butter or margarine
1½ cups thinly sliced onions
1½ teaspoons salt

¼ teaspoon black pepper
1 teaspoon wine vinegar
1 tablespoon minced parsley

- Melt 3 tablespoons of butter in a frying pan; sauté onions until delicately browned; remove.
- Melt remaining butter and brown beef on both sides.
- Return onions and season with salt and pepper.
- Cook over low heat 5 minutes, turning filets once.
- Sprinkle with the vinegar and parsley.

STEAK WITH GARLIC OIL   Serves 4

steak (12 oz. per person)
2 cloves garlic

1 cup olive oil
salt and pepper to taste

- Have meat cut from ¾ to 1 inch thick, gash around the edge about every 4 inches to prevent curling.
- Put garlic to soak in oil the night before. Pour the oil into a shallow pan, remove the garlic and dip the steak in the oil, coating both sides.
- Place the steak on the grill. When it is nearly done, season with salt and pepper.

SKEWERED HAMBURGER

Serves 6

garlic, finely chopped
salt and pepper
½ cup olive oil

1 pound ground beef
½ cup finely chopped onion

- Combine all ingredients thoroughly.
- Take barbecue skewers and form meat around skewers to about 1½ inch diameter. Length of meat along skewer may be varied to suit size of buns to be used.
- Barbecue over charcoal, turning continuously to keep juices in.
- Push meat off skewers into buns and serve with mustard and catsup.

Variation:

HAMBURGER EN BROCHETTE

- Form seasoned meat mixture into balls the size of a small egg; string 2 or 3 meat balls on skewers, alternating with onion and quarters of unpeeled tomato.
- Sprinkle with salt or brush with barbecue sauce; grill until done.

STUFFED FLANK STEAK

Serves 6

2 pounds flank steak (½-inch thick)
2 cups seasoned bread stuffing
1½ to 2 tablespoons fat
1 teaspoon salt

⅛ teaspoon pepper
2 tablespoons flour
1 teaspoon paprika
1½ cups beef broth

- Snip edge of steak, score well.
- Spread with stuffing; roll and skewer or tie; brown well in fat over moderate heat about 15 minutes.
- Add salt and pepper, sprinkle with flour and brown lightly again.
- Add paprika and broth, stir well; cover, cook slowly on top of stove or in 325°F. oven 1 to 1¼ hours, turn once.
- Remove skewers or string, slice the roll; serve with gravy.

STEAK ITALIAN STYLE

Serves 4

1¼ pounds top round beef, cut in
1½ x 4 inch strips
salt and pepper

garlic, minced
grated Romano cheese

- Sprinkle each piece of meat with salt, pepper, minced garlic, and Romano cheese.
- Roll up and skewer on toothpicks.
- Broil 5 minutes on each side.

STEAK HAWAIIAN

1 clove garlic, finely chopped   Steak, sirloin, round
½ to 1 cup soy sauce

- Place garlic in a large shallow glass baking dish. Add soy sauce. Marinate steak for 15 minutes, turning frequently to thoroughly impregnate the meat with seasoning. Then barbecue to taste.

SWISS STEAK   Serves 6

2 pounds round OR flank steak   2 tablespoons flour
  (½ to ¾ inch thick)   2½ cups canned or stewed tomatoes
1 small onion, sliced   1 teaspoon Worcestershire sauce
1 teaspoon salt   1 tablespoon chopped celery
⅛ teaspoon pepper   1 tablespoon chopped green pepper

- Snip fat edge of steak; pound meat on both sides; brown well.
- Brown sliced onion, add salt and pepper; sprinkle both sides with flour and brown again lightly.
- Add remaining ingredients, stir well; add more liquid during cooking if necessary.
- Cover, cook slowly on top of stove or in 325°F. oven 1¼ to 1½ hours, turn once during cooking.

TERIYAKI STEAK   Serves 6

1 clove garlic, mashed   ½ cup soy sauce
1½ teaspoons ginger   4 tablespoons dry white table wine
1 tablespoon sugar   2 pounds top round steak
1 tablespoon cider vinegar

- Mash garlic with ginger in a bowl.
- Dissolve sugar in vinegar; combine with garlic and ginger, add soy and wine.
- Marinate steaks in this liquid for several hours, turning occasionally. Grill steaks as desired.

⇌VEAL SECTION⇌

CREOLE VEAL STEAK
Serves 6 - 8

3 tablespoons butter or margarine
3 pounds veal steak, cut in
  serving-sized pieces
2 teaspoons salt
¾ teaspoon black pepper
½ pound ham, diced
3 sweet potatoes, peeled and sliced
2 tablespoons olive oil
1½ cups chopped onion

1 clove garlic, minced
2 cups canned tomatoes,
  drained and chopped
¼ teaspoon cayenne pepper
3 tablespoons minced parsley
¼ teaspoon thyme
1 bay leaf, crushed
1 package frozen okra, sliced

- Melt butter over medium heat; brown veal on both sides.
- Season with 1 teaspoon salt and the pepper.
- Add ham and sweet potatoes; cover and cook over low heat 20 minutes.
- Meanwhile heat oil in saucepan; brown onions and garlic; add tomatoes, cayenne pepper, parsley, thyme, bay leaf and remaining salt; bring to a boil and cook over low heat 10 minutes; add to veal; cover and cook 30 minutes.
- Add okra; cook 20 minutes longer.

VEAL CHOPS PARMIGIANA
Serves 4

½ cup fine dry bread crumbs
½ cup grated Parmesan cheese
¾ teaspoon salt
¾ teaspoon paprika
4 large loin veal chops
  (2 - 2½ pounds)

1 egg, beaten
3 tablespoons butter or margarine
4 thin slices Mozzarella cheese
2 cups well-seasoned tomato sauce

- Mix first 4 ingredients; dip chops into egg and roll in crumb mixture.
- Brown chops on both sides in butter, cover each with a slice of Mozzarella.
- Pour tomato sauce over chops, cover and simmer for about 45 minutes. (If sauce is too thick, add a little hot water).

VEAL CUTLET PAPRIKA   Serves 4

2 pounds veal cutlet about   6 tablespoons butter or margarine
    ¾ inch thick   1 tablespoon paprika
    salt and pepper   ½ cup dry white wine
    flour   1 cup sour cream

- Season cutlet with salt and pepper; dredge with flour.
- Sauté slowly in butter until browned on both sides.
- Add paprika, sprinkling it over surface of meat; add wine, cover and simmer slowly about ½ hour.
- Remove meat to hot platter; add one teaspoon paprika, stir in 1 cup sour cream.
- Pour sauce over veal; serve at once with buttered noodles.

VEAL CUTLET PROVENCALE   Serves 4

2 pounds veal steak   ½ cup red wine
½ cup olive oil   2 tablespoons chopped parsley
2 cloves garlic, chopped   12 ripe olives
2 tomatoes, peeled, seeded,
    finely chopped

- Season veal steak, dredge with flour.
- Sauté slowly in oil until browned on both sides.
- Add garlic, cover and cook for 10 minutes, simmering over low heat.
- Add tomatoes and red wine, cover and allow to simmer until tender.
- Just before serving, add chopped parsley and olives; remove the meat to a platter and mix the sauce well; pour over veal. Serve with rice baked in the oven.

VEAL SCALOPPINE WITH MARSALA   Serves 4 - 6

1½ pounds veal cutlet, cut in   ½ teaspoon black pepper
    16 pieces, pounded thin   2 tablespoons butter
½ cup flour   2 tablespoons olive oil
2 teaspoons salt   ⅓ cup Marsala

- Dip each piece of veal in a mixture of flour, salt and pepper.
- Brown on both sides in melted butter over high heat.
- Add wine, bring to a boil, cook over medium heat 2 minutes.

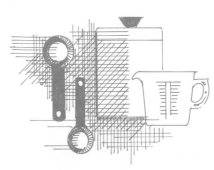

⋟ LAMB SECTION ⋞

BAKED LAMB CHOPS   Serves 6

6 loin lamb chops, 1½ inches thick
6 small slices of liverwurst
    OR
6 teaspoons liver pâté

2 almonds slivered
freshly ground pepper and nutmeg
onion juice or finely chopped onion
segments of orange, optional

- Cut a slit in the side of each chop where the meat is thickest without breaking into either surface.
- Into each slit insert 1 slice of liverwurst and slivered almonds; fasten opening with toothpicks.
- Sprinkle both sides of each chop with pepper, nutmeg and onion juice.
- Bake, uncovered, in 425°F. oven for 30 minutes.
- Garnish with orange segments.

BAKED LAMB CHOPS WITH RICE   Serves 6

6 lean loin lamb chops
1 tablespoon butter or margarine
    salt and pepper
½ cup water
1 cup tomato sauce

¼ cup catsup
1 tablespoon Worcestershire sauce
¼ teaspoon garlic powder
½ teaspoon dried oregano
    cooked rice

- Brown lamb chops in butter and place in a casserole; sprinkle with salt and pepper.
- Pour water into pan; stir to loosen drippings; add remaining ingredients, except rice, pour over chops.
- Cover and bake in 350°F. oven for 1 hour; serve with rice.

BARBECUED LAMB   Serves 6

3 pounds lamb, bone-in (shank, breast, neck slices, flank) OR
2 pounds boneless flank
1/2 cup water

1 1/2 cups sliced onions
1 1/2 cups sliced carrots
3 cups tomato juice
2 tablespoons Worcestershire sauce

- Cut meat in serving-size pieces, brown well on all sides; drain.
- Add water, onions and carrots; cover and cook slowly on top of stove or in a 325°F. oven 30 minutes.
- Pour off fat and liquid; add last 2 ingredients; cover and continue cooking 1 to 1 1/4 hours.
- Uncover for last 30 minutes of cooking.

BARBECUED RIBLETS   Serves 6

- Cut 3 pounds lamb riblets in 2 rib pieces.
- Place on rack in shallow roasting pan; bake in 425°F. oven 30 minutes; pour off fat.
- Cover riblets with 3 cups barbecue sauce; reduce to 325°F. and bake 1 hour, basting frequently.

DEVILED LAMB CHOPS   Serves 8

1 tablespoon olive oil
1/2 teaspoon salt
1/2 teaspoon pepper
1/2 teaspoon oregano
1 clove garlic, minced
8 loin lamb chops, cut 1 inch thick

4 anchovy fillets, chopped
1/2 teaspoon oregano
1/2 teaspoon salt
1/8 teaspoon black pepper
2 teaspoons lemon juice
1 tablespoon prepared mustard

- Mix together first six ingredients; rub into chops and let stand at room temperature 2 hours.
- Mix together remaining ingredients; arrange chops on an oiled broiling pan; brush tops with the anchovy mixture.
- Broil in a hot broiler 10 minutes; turn over, brush chops with anchovy mixture again and broil 10 minutes or to desired degree of doneness, baste frequently.

LAMB CHOPS WITH MUSTARD   Serves 4

4 lamb chops, cut 1 1/2 inches thick
1 1/4 teaspoons salt
1/4 teaspoon black pepper

3 tablespoons prepared mustard
2 tablespoons honey

- Season chops with salt and pepper.
- Broil 10 minutes on 1 side, then turn over and broil 8 minutes.
- Mix together the mustard and honey; spread over chops and broil 2 minutes longer.

LAMB KABOBS
Serves 6

1 pound boneless lamb, cubed
2 tablespoons salad oil
2 tablespoons vinegar
½ teaspoon mustard
1 teaspoon salt

1 clove garlic, minced
1 teaspoon curry powder
3 medium tomatoes, quartered
12 whole, pickled onions
12 medium mushroom caps

- Let meat stand 1 hour in marinade of salad oil, vinegar, mustard, salt, garlic and curry powder.
- Make 6 kabobs by placing alternate pieces of lamb, mushrooms, tomatoes and onion.
- Brush vegetables with oil; sprinkle with salt and pepper.
- Broil kabobs in pre-heated broiler 3 inches from heat, 5 to 7 minutes per side.

LAMB SHISH-KABOB
Serves 4

2 pounds shoulder lamb chops,
  1½ inches thick
8 small onions, peeled
2 medium green peppers, cut
  into eighths
4 tomatoes, quartered

½ cup cooking oil
1 teaspoon salt
¼ teaspoon pepper
1 teaspoon marjoram
2 teaspoons fresh lemon juice

- Bone chops and cut meat into cubes.
- Put meat and vegetables in bowl; mix remaining ingredients and add; store in refrigerator for at least 1 hour before cooking.
- Alternate meat and vegetables on skewers.
- Cook over hot coals, turing to brown all sides, about 10 to 15 minutes.

PORK SECTION

BAKED PORK CHOPS ORIENTAL STYLE   Serves 8

1 cup soy sauce
¼ cup sherry
2 pieces crystallized ginger

2 chopped green onions
8 thick pork chops

- Boil first 4 ingredients together with 1 cup water. Place pork chops in marinade in refrigerator for several hours.
- Remove from the refrigerator ½ hour before cooking. Bake 1 hour in the marinade in 300°F. oven.

BAKED STUFFED PORK CHOPS   Serves 6

6 loin pork chops, cut
  1½ inches thick
5 cups toasted fresh bread crumbs
½ cup chopped green olives
1 cup whole-kernel corn, drained
3 tablespoons grated onion
1 teaspoon celery salt

1 cup beef broth
1½ teaspoons Worcestershire sauce
1 teaspoon salt
½ teaspoon black pepper
¼ cup flour
12 pimiento-stuffed olives

- Slit chops through the middle, from the outer edges to the bone.
- Mix together next 7 ingredients and stuff chops, closing the openings with toothpicks or skewers; reserve the remaining stuffing.
- Season chops with salt and pepper, dip lightly in the flour; arrange chops in a greased baking dish.
- Bake in a 350°F. oven 35 minutes, drain, turn chops and spread remaining stuffing in dish.
- Bake 40 minutes longer or until chops are tender.
- Garnish with whole olives.

BROILED PORK   Serves 6

2 pounds lean pork, cut
  into ¾ inch cubes
½ cup soy sauce
¼ cup saké or white wine

2 tablespoons sugar
1 clove garlic, crushed
½ ounce fresh gingerroot, sliced

- Marinate meat in rest of ingredients for 1 hour, broil over charcoal or in a broiler, basting with the marinade and turning so that all sides become brown and shiny.
- Cook until pork is thoroughly done but not dry, for 20 to 25 minutes.

CHARCOAL BROILED HAM STEAKS   Serves 3-4

1 slice ham steak, ½ to ¾ inch thick
3 teaspoons dry mustard
¾ cup brown sugar

½ cup juice from a can of sliced
  pineapple
3 slices canned pineapple

- Put steak on grill and baste with a thin paste of the mustard, brown sugar, and pineapple juice. Use mustard sparingly at first, then add more to taste.
- Remove steak when brown. Put pineapple rings on grill until steaming brown, serve them on top of the steak.

CHEF'S SPARERIBS   Serves 4

¼ cup brown sugar
2 teaspoons salt
1 tablespoon celery seed
1 tablespoon chili powder

1 teaspoon paprika
3 pounds pork spareribs
¼ cup vinegar
1 cup canned tomato sauce

- Mix dry ingredients and rub part of the mixture into the ribs.
- Combine remainder of mixture with the vinegar and tomato sauce for basting.
- Let ribs stand for an hour or longer, then spread on grill over slow fire, basting occasionally with sauce.
- To reduce cooking time, pre-cook ribs in kitchen oven until almost tender, then finish on barbecue grill.

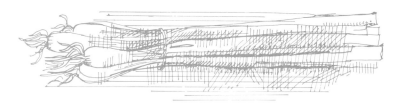

CHINESE FRIED PORK WITH GREEN ONIONS   Serves 4

1 pound boneless pork, cut paper
  thin, cut in 1 inch squares
¼ cup soy sauce
2 tablespoons dry sherry

3 tablespoons vegetable oil
2 bunches green onions, cut
  into 2 inch pieces
1 teaspoon salt

- Toss meat with the soya sauce and sherry, let stand 20 minutes.
- Sauté pork in hot oil until no pink remains, stir frequently.
- Add green onions and salt; cook over high heat 30 seconds, stirring constantly.

HAM WITH PINEAPPLE SAUCE

- Broil thin slices of ham on the grill. When slightly brown, begin basting with pineapple sauce and continue until ham is tender and well seasoned.

Basting sauce:

1 cup brown sugar
½ cup vinegar

2 tablespoons dry mustard
1 cup pineapple juice

- Cook the sugar, vinegar, and mustard together slowly for 3 minutes. Remove from the heat, add the pineapple juice.

HAM WITH BAKED ONION AND PEANUTS   Serves 4

1 inch slice cooked ham, baked
   or pan fried
3½ cups sliced onions
2 tablespoons butter or margarine

3 tablespoons flour
¾ cup milk
1 cup peanuts, chopped

- Cook the onions in a little water until tender, drain and save half the liquid.
- Make a cream sauce: Melt the butter, add the flour, stirring until smooth.
- Add the onion liquid and milk, stirring until smooth and thickened.
- Mix with the onions and put a layer in the bottom of a buttered baking dish.
- Sprinkle with peanuts and repeat the layers, topping with peanuts.
- Bake until browned on top, about 25 minutes.
- Serve with cooked ham slice.

POOR MAN'S BARBECUED HAM SLICES

1 tablespoon dry mustard
½ tablespoon powdered ginger
1 cup spiced peach syrup (or any
   spiced fruit syrup)

Ham slices, cut ¼ to ⅜ inch thick
(as many as you want)

- Make a paste of the dry mustard and ginger by adding the syrup slowly. Stir until a smooth sauce results.
- Paint ham slices on one side with the sauce. Place on grill, sauce side down, about 12 inches above a slow charcoal fire. Paint the top side of the ham. Turn the ham often and keep moist with the sauce.
- *Don't be in a hurry!* Keep over slow fire for at least 30 to 40 minutes. Don't let the slices rest on one side too long. Turn them often, let them brown, not burn, use all of the sauce.

PINEAPPLE SPARERIBS   Serves 6

2 racks spareribs, cut in
  individual ribs
8 cups water
1½ cups cider vinegar
1 cup sifted cornstarch
¼ cup dark molasses

¼ cup soy sauce
1 cup cooking oil
20 ounce can pineapple chunks
⅓ cup sugar
2 green peppers, cut in strips

• Bring 7 cups of water to a boil; add ½ cup of vinegar and the ribs; bring to a boil again and cook over medium heat 15 minutes; drain, cool ribs.

• Brown ribs in hot oil; drain.

• Blend cornstarch, molasses, soy sauce; coat ribs with all of the mixture.

• Drain the pineapple, reserving ¾ cup of juice.

• Bring to a boil sugar, pineapple juice, remaining water and vinegar; add ribs, cover and cook over low heat 25 minutes, turning the ribs frequently.

• Add green pepper and pineapple; cook 5 minutes longer.

PORK CHOPS WITH APPLES   Serves 4

2 pounds cooking apples, peeled,
  cored, cut in 1 inch slices
2 tablespoons lemon juice
  flour
4 slices bacon

8 loin pork chops, cut
  ½ inch thick
1½ teaspoons salt
½ teaspoon black pepper
½ cup sugar

• Sprinkle apple slices with lemon juice and dip lightly in flour.

• Cook bacon until crisp, then drain, crumble and reserve.

• Pour off all but 2 tablespoons fat and reserve.

• Brown pork chops on both sides in remaining fat, cover and cook until done, about 15 minutes.

• Season with salt and pepper, remove and keep hot.

• Add 2 tablespoons of reserved fat to pan, fry apple slices until browned on both sides, sprinkle both sides with sugar and cook until glazed.

• Arrange pork chops on a heated platter with apple slices around them, sprinkle with bacon.

PORK CHOPS WITH POTATO STUFFING   Serves 4

¾ cup dry bread crumbs
2 tablespoons butter or margarine
½ cup finely chopped celery
⅓ cup finely chopped onion

1½ cups mashed potatoes
1 egg
salt and pepper
4 thick loin pork chops

- Sauté the bread crumbs, celery, and onion in the butter.
- Add parsley and mix with the mashed potatoes, egg, and seasonings.
- Sauté chops on one side, turn so that the cooked side is up.
- Pile the cooked side with the potato mixture.
- Arrange in a shallow casserole and bake in a 350°F. oven about one hour, basting from time to time with the pork juice.

PORK CHOPS WITH SAUERKRAUT GARNISH   Serves 6

6 thick slices bacon
4 cups sauerkraut, rinsed and drained
6 pork chops, about ¾ inch thick
1 medium onion, sliced

12 peppercorns
6 strips pimiento
2 cups chicken bouillon and
1 cup white dry wine OR
3 cups chicken bouillon

- Arrange bacon in bottom of large, deep frying pan; top with sauerkraut and pork chops.
- Combine remaining ingredients; pour over chops; cover and simmer for about 1 hour.

ROASTED SAVORY SPARERIBS

- Select as many sides of spareribs as required and have the butcher crack them down the middle. Cut between the ribs into serving-size pieces. Rub each piece well with a mixture of 2 tablespoons sage to 1 cup flour.
- Place the ribs over charcoal fire and cook slowly for 45 minutes to 1 hour.
- Turn frequently and brush often with a sauce made by combining the following ingredients.

Sauce:

1 teaspoon garlic powder
¾ teaspoon onion salt
½ teaspoon freshly ground pepper
½ teaspoon seasoned salt

1 teaspoon dry mustard
⅓ cup olive oil
½ cup vinegar
1½ cups cold water

SPARERIBS WITH ONION

Sweet onions, chopped fine
Pork spareribs, cracked

Salt and pepper
Butter to sauté onions

- Spread finely chopped onions on spareribs, roll up with onions inside and place in refrigerator or cooler overnight. Just before barbecuing, scrape off onions and season meat with salt and freshly ground pepper. Sauté onions in butter and serve with spareribs.

SPICY SPARERIBS   Serves 2

2 pounds spareribs
1 cup tomato sauce
4 whole cloves
⅛ cinnamon stick
1 stalk celery, chopped fine
    or
¼ teaspoon celery salt
1 clove garlic minced

2 dashes Tabasco sauce
1 tablespoon steak sauce
2 tablespoon vinegar
1 tablespoon sugar
½ teaspoon chili powder
2 tablespoons chutney
⅛ teaspoon dry mustard
1 small onion, chopped fine

- Leave ribs in one piece. Cook all other ingredients for 20 minutes or until blended to taste. Baste ribs frequently with this sauce during barbecuing.

STUFFED PORK TENDERLOIN   Serves 6

2 pork tenderloins
  (about 1 pound each)
2 large apples, peeled, chopped
  salt and pepper

12 cooked prunes, pitted
2 tablespoons butter or margarine
½ cup beef bouillon
1 cup heavy cream

- Split tenderloins lengthwise, cutting two thirds through; open flat and pound to an even thickness.
- Place apples on meat and sprinkle with salt and pepper.
- Lay prunes across the short end of each tenderloin, roll like a jelly roll; tie securely; brown on all sides in butter.
- Add bouillon and heavy cream; cover and simmer for 1 hour, stirring occasionally. (Add water if necessary).
- Remove meat to hot platter, skim fat from sauce; reheat and pour over meat.

TOMATO PORK TENDERLOIN   Serves 4

1 large pork tenderloin, sliced in
  2 inch pieces, flattened
2 tablespoons all-purpose flour
3 tablespoons shortening
1 small onion, chopped

1 clove garlic, minced
1 beef or chicken bouillon cube
1 cup water
½ cup tomato juice

- Season meat with salt and pepper, roll in flour.
- Brown on both sides in shortening; remove and lightly brown onion and garlic in drippings.
- Add remaining ingredients and bring to boil, stirring constantly.
- Return pork to skillet, cover, simmer 30 minutes.

POULTRY SECTION

BAKED CHICKEN SUPREME

Serves 6

1 can condensed cream of
   mushroom soup
2 tablespoons minced parsley
1 tablespoon minced green onion

1 clove garlic, minced
½ teaspoon crushed tarragon
   dash thyme
3 chicken breasts, halved

- Combine first 6 ingredients; spread on surface and in cavity of chicken breasts.
- Place each breast on square of foil; seal; fold corners under; place on cooky sheet.
- Bake in 450°F. oven about 40 to 45 minutes, turning once.

BARBECUED CHICKEN PAPRIKA

Serves 4

2 fryers or broilers (about 1½ to
   2 pounds each)
1½ cups olive oil or cooking oil

2 cloves garlic, minced
4 tablespoons paprika
   salt and pepper

- Quarter chicken, wash quickly, dry well; place in shallow pan. Mix together the oil, garlic, and paprika, pour over chicken. Marinate 3 to 4 hours, turning chicken about every half hour.
- Season with salt and pepper and place quarters on grill. Broil over hot coals, baste frequently with the marinade.

BREADED CHICKEN PARTS

Serves 4

3 pound chicken, cut up
2 eggs

¼ cup fine dry bread crumbs
⅓ cup honey

- Dry chicken pieces thoroughly with paper toweling.
- Beat eggs with about 2 tablespoons of water, fine bread crumbs and salt.
- With a pastry brush, brush the chicken pieces with honey on both sides, then dip into the egg and bread crumb mixture, coating thoroughly.
- Arrange in a shallow, baking dish; bake at 325°F. oven for about 1½ hours.

BROILED TURKEY OR CHICKEN

turkey for broiling
½ pound butter or margarine
1 teaspoon paprika
1 teaspoon black pepper

few drops lemon juice
pinch of tarragon
salt and pepper

- Have the turkey split and cleaned, saving the giblets for the sauce.
- Cream 1 cup butter with paprika, black pepper, lemon juice and tarragon; spread over the surface and place bone side down over the fire, which should not be too hot.
- Cook about 15 minutes and then turn the skin side to the fire.
- Baste and let it cook on that side about 10 minutes before turning and buttering again.
- Keep turning at intervals of about 5 minutes until the bird is cooked through, but not dry.
- Baste with butter each time, being very careful not to puncture the skin.

BROILED SPLIT TURKEY   Serves 8

- Split a 6-8 pound turkey down the back, remove breastbone so it can flatten out like a thick steak. Have at hand a bowl of melted butter or margarine, mixed with a little chopped garlic and parsley. Broil the turkey like a steak over a deep bed of coals. Baste liberally with the melted butter.
- Keep a bowl of water at hand. When flames spring up, sprinkle water (don't splash) on flames. By sprinkling lightly you create little steam clouds. After 45-60 minutes of this alternate steaming and broiling and frequent turnings you will have a broiled fowl ready to eat.

BARBECUED WILD DUCK   Serves 8

¾ cup olive oil
½ cup vinegar
¼ cup soy sauce
3 cloves garlic, mashed
1 sprig rosemary

1 tablespoon celery seeds
1 teaspoon salt
¼ teaspoon pepper
4 pintails (or other wild ducks)

- Combine all sauce ingredients, simmer 10 minutes to blend flavours.
- Cut ducks into halves and barbecue, turning several times and brushing with sauce generously, about 45-60 minutes.

BROILED DUCK   Serves 2

1 duck (2 to 3½ pounds)
¾ cup prepared French dressing
1 teaspoon dry mustard

2 teaspoons Worcestershire sauce
2 teaspoons grated orange peel
1 teaspoon grated lemon peel

- Split duck up backbone with poultry shears. Place breast side down on meat cutting board and break down breast bones by pressing with another board or by pounding gently with a meat tenderizing mallet.
- Mix the sauce ingredients together and use mixture to baste the duck liberally. Insert the duck in a hinged wire grill and broil over hot coals until done to taste, basting it at least once more while cooking, 10 minutes a side; or as desired. Divide duck at breastbone into two portions and serve.

CHICKEN IN YOGHURT SAUCE   Serves 4

2½-3 pound chicken, cut up
1 cup water
2 tablespoons butter or margarine
2 medium onions, chopped
1 tablespoon flour

1 cup yoghurt
1 teaspoon grated lemon peel
salt, pepper
mashed potatoes
walnut halves

- Sauté chicken in butter until golden brown.
- Add onions, salt and pepper, and 1 cup of water.
- Cover tightly, simmer over low heat until tender, about 25-30 minutes.
- Mix the flour with the yoghurt and lemon peel, pour over chicken.
- Stir well until this mixture is mixed with the juices from the chicken.
- Simmer about 10 minutes more, serve surrounded with a ring of mashed potatoes; arrange walnut halves at intervals on mashed potatoes.

CHICKEN ITALIAN STYLE   Serves 4

3 tablespoons melted butter or
  margarine
1 tablespoon oil
3 pound broiler-fryer chicken,
  cut into serving pieces

¾ cup fine dry bread crumbs
1 teaspoon oregano leaves
1 teaspoon paprika
½ teaspoon salt
¼ teaspoon garlic powder

- Combine butter and oil, and brush chicken pieces.
- Combine remaining ingredients; roll chicken in crumb mixture.
- Arrange in 13 x 9 x 2 inch baking pan.
- Bake in 350°F. oven about 1½ hours or until chicken is tender.

CHICKEN SUKIYAKI

Serves 2

1 tablespoon soy sauce
2 tablespoons orange juice
1 teaspoon sugar
  dash salt
1 whole chicken breast, deboned

2 teaspoons oil
½ cup diagonally sliced celery
2 onions, sliced thin
¾ cup sliced mushrooms

- Combine soy sauce, juice, sugar and salt. Bring to a boil, cool.
- Cut chicken into 2 x 1 x ½ inch strips.
- Sauté in oil for 1 minute.
- Add vegetables and sauce, cook 7 minutes more.
- Serve over rice.

CRISPY OVEN-FRIED CHICKEN

- Cut chicken into serving pieces, wash and pat dry.
- Sprinkle with salt and pepper; dip pieces in melted butter or margarine; roll pieces in crumbs; place pieces in well-greased shallow baking pan and drizzle with melted butter.
- Bake in 325°F. oven for 1 hour or until chicken is tender.

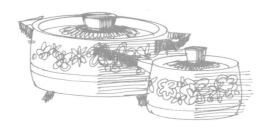

CREOLE FRIED CHICKEN

Serves 6

2 2½ pound fryers
2 eggs
½ cup milk
1½ cups dry bread crumbs

¾ cup flour
salt and pepper
fat

- Cut chickens into serving pieces.
- Beat eggs slightly and mix with milk; pour the egg-and-milk mixture over chicken pieces; let stand 2 hours.
- Mix crumbs and flour with salt and pepper.
- Heat fat in large frying pan to a depth of 1½ inches.
- Dip chicken pieces into crumb-and-flour mixture; place in hot fat; brown quickly on both sides, then cook, covered, for 10 minutes; uncover and cook until tender.
- When tender, drain on absorbent paper; arrange on platter; serve with cream gravy, boiled rice, sautéed corn and hot biscuits.

CURRIED DUCK

Serves 4

5-6 pound duck
2 teaspoons Worcestershire sauce
1 tablespoon curry
   salt and pepper
¼ cup duck fat

1 clove garlic
⅓ cup finely chopped onion
1½ cups duck broth
¼ cup flour

- Cut duck in serving-size pieces, discarding backbone, neck, wing tips, and skin. Cook the discarded pieces and giblets in 3 cups of boiling salted water about 45 minutes.
- Strain the broth and chill until the fat rises to the top, lift it off carefully and save.
- Chop the neck meat and giblets.
- Rub the pieces of duck with Worcestershire sauce, curry powder, salt and pepper.
- Heat the duck fat in a Dutch oven over medium heat.
- Add the pieces of duck, brown lightly on both sides.
- Add the garlic and onion, cook for 2 minutes, add ¾ cup of duck broth, cover tightly, and cook over low heat until duck is tender, about 45 minutes.
- Mix the remaining duck broth and flour, add to the pot, and cook until the sauce thickens, stirring constantly.
- Serve over the rice.

CURRIED TURKEY

Serves 4

4 1 pound turkey legs
¼ cup vegetable oil
1 large onion, chopped
1 clove of garlic, minced
2 teaspoons curry powder
¾ teaspoon salt
½ teaspoon ground ginger

water
2 tablespoons lemon juice
2 cups applesauce
1 6 ounce package chicken-flavoured
   rice mix
   butter or margarine

- Brown turkey legs slowly in oil in a heavy kettle or Dutch oven; remove.
- Stir onion, garlic, curry powder, salt and ginger into drippings in kettle; cook slowly until onion is soft.
- Stir in 1½ cups water, lemon juice and applesauce.
- Return turkey to kettle; heat to boiling; cover.
- Simmer, turning turkey several times, about 2 hours.
- Cook rice mix with water and butter or margarine, following label directions.
- Place turkey in the center of a heated serving platter; spoon rice at each end.
- Skim fat, if any, from sauce in kettle; reheat sauce to boiling. Serve separately.

LOW CALORIE FRIED CHICKEN

- Cut chicken into serving pieces, wash and pat dry.
- Sprinkle pieces with salt and pepper; dip pieces into milk and roll in crumbs, coating each piece well.
- Place pieces in well-greased shallow baking pan; bake in 325°F. oven for 1 hour or until chicken is tender.

MANDARIN ORANGE CHICKEN BREASTS　　　Serves 6

6 12 ounce half chicken breasts, boned
salt
1½ cups hot cooked rice
3 tablespoons butter or margarine
1½ tablespoon chopped parsley
¼ teaspoon leaf rosemary, crumbed
¼ teaspoon leaf basil, crumbed
¼ cup flour
1 teaspoon paprika

2 envelopes instant chicken broth
1¾ cups water
1 tablespoon instant minced onion
2 tablespoons lemon juice
1 bay leaf
1 tablespoon cornstarch
1 cup mandarin orange segments, drained
1 cup seedless green grapes

- Sprinkle insides of chicken breast lightly with salt.
- Combine rice, 1 tablespoon of the butter, ¼ teaspoon salt, parsley, rosemary and basil in a large bowl; toss lightly to mix; spoon into hollows in chicken breasts. Fold edges over stuffing to cover completely; fasten with wooden picks.
- Mix flour, paprika and ½ teaspoon salt in a pie plate; dip chicken breasts into mixture to coat well. Brown slowly in remaining 2 tablespoons butter.
- Stir in chicken broth, water, onion, lemon juice and bay leaf; heat to boiling; cover.
- Simmer 25 minutes, or until chicken is tender; remove bay leaf. Place chicken on a heated serving platter; keep warm. Reheat liquid to boiling.
- Mix cornstarch with a little water to form paste; stir into liquid in frying pan. Cook, stirring constantly, until sauce thickens and boils, 3 minutes.
- Stir in mandarin orange segments and grapes; heat until bubbly.
- Spoon over chicken. Garnish with additional grapes and mandarin orange segments.

MARINATED BROILED CHICKEN   Serves 6

2 1½ pound broiler-fryers
¾ cup vegetable oil
¾ cup tarragon vinegar

3 tablespoons hot prepared mustard
½ teaspoon seasoned salt
½ teaspoon seasoned pepper

- Remove giblets and necks from chicken packages and save to make chicken broth. Cut chickens into serving-size pieces.
- Combine oil, vinegar, mustard, salt and pepper; add chicken.
- Marinate 2 hours (in refrigerator), turning once.
- Place chicken, skin side down, on broiler rack.
- Broil, 6 inches from heat, 15 minutes; turn.
- Broil 20 to 30 minutes longer, basting frequently, or until chicken is tender.

SAUTEED LEMON CHICKEN   Serves 4

2½-3 pound broiler-fryer
3 tablespoons butter or margarine
1 teaspoon salt

½ teaspoon leaf rosemary,
   crumbled
1 lemon, sliced and seeded

- Cut chicken into serving-size pieces.
- Heat butter slowly in a large, heavy frying pan, add all the chicken pieces and brown slowly, 10 minutes on each side.
- Sprinkle with salt and rosemary, arrange lemon slices over chicken pieces and cover.
- Simmer 20 minutes, or until chicken is tender. (Check after 10 minutes and if liquid from lemon slices has evaporated, add ¼ cup water to prevent scorching.)

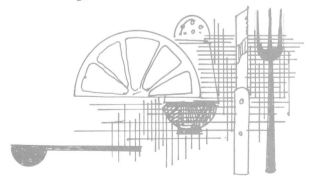

SAVOURY FRIED CHICKEN   Serves 4

2½ pound broiler-fryer
2 eggs
¾ cup flour
1 teaspoon salt
1 teaspoon basil
½ teaspoon thyme
½ teaspoon pepper
¼ teaspoon ground nutmeg
Shortening or vegetable oil

- Cut chicken into serving-size pieces.
- Beat eggs in a shallow dish. Combine flour, salt, basil, thyme, pepper and nutmeg in a plastic bag.
- Dip chicken pieces in eggs, allowing excess to drip off; shake in flour mixture to coat well.
- Dip again in egg and shake in flour mixture to form a thick coating.
- Place chicken pieces on wire rack for 15 minutes to allow coating to set.
- Melt enough shortening, or pour enough oil into a large heavy frying pan.
- Place over medium heat. When a few drops of water sizzle when flicked into the hot fat, add the chicken pieces, skin-side down. Cook slowly, turning once, 20 minutes, or until chicken is golden.
- Reduce heat; cover skillet. Cook 30 minutes longer, or until chicken is tender. Remove cover for last 5 minutes for a crisp crust.

SPIT-ROASTED TURKEY

- Select a turkey weighing 10 to 12 pounds; wash and dry.
- Sprinkle cavity with salt and a little thyme or marjoram, add a stalk of celery and a few slices of onion; truss securely having both wings and legs close to body and neck skin skewered on at back.
- Drive spit from a point just in front of the tail, having it go through the back and come out at about the top of the wishbone.
- Rub skin with cooking oil; insert a meat thermometer in the thickest part of the thigh.
- Connect spit to the motor and roast over medium heat until meat thermometer registers 175°F. or until leg moves easily in joint; allow about 15 minutes cooking time for each pound of bird; baste frequently with melted margarine as it turns.

SWEET AND SOUR CHICKEN   Serves 6

1 frying chicken (3½ pounds) cut up	3 peppercorns
2 cups water	2 teaspoons salt
juice of 1 lime	¼ cup butter or margarine
1 clove garlic	1 cup firmly packed brown sugar
1 teaspoon oregano	¼ cup vinegar

- Wash chicken in mixture of water and lime juice; drain and dry on absorbent paper.
- Mash garlic with the seasonings; rub well into both sides of chicken pieces.
- Melt butter; add chicken and brown quickly on both sides; add remaining ingredients.
- As soon as sugar melts, turn heat to low, cover and cook for 30 minutes.
- Uncover, turn chicken pieces and cook for 30 minutes longer, or until chicken is tender.

TURKEY STEAKS

- Buy a large, hard-frozen, eviscerated turkey — the bigger the better. Ask your butcher to cut it on his power saw into 1-inch transverse slices, starting at the front of the breastbone, and working back to about where the thighs join the body. If you're serving a large number of people, have him cut more slices — one slice will make two good servings. The two ends that are left can be kept frozen until you need them.
- Lay the frozen slices in a large flat pan (you can stack them), drizzle enough cooking oil to coat each one.
- As the slices thaw, the oil and juices will make a fine marinade in the pan.
- This should be brushed back over the slices from time to time. When completely thawed, divide each slice into two steaks with a sharp, heavy knife. (The cross sections of breast and backbone will split easily.)
- Arrange steaks in toasting racks, brush with basting sauce (¼ pound butter, ½ cup dry white wine, salt, and pepper). Broil about 8 inches from a hot fire for 10 minutes on each side. Turn a couple of times, and brush with more butter-wine mixture.
- Serve with the remainder of the basting sauce heated and spooned over each serving.

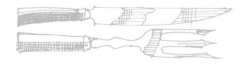

⤳VARIETY MEAT SECTION⤳

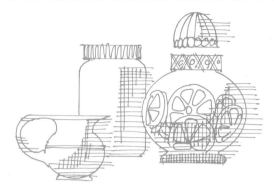

BAKED BRATWURST
Serves 4

1 pound bratwurst
⅓ cup chili sauce
1 tablespoon chopped parsley
1 tablespoon instant minced onion

¼ cup chopped celery
⅓ cup pickle liquid
¼ cup chopped pickles or pickle relish
baked beans

- Prick bratwurst and arrange in shallow baking dish.
- Combine next 6 ingredients and pour over top.
- Bake in 350°F. oven for 30 minutes; serve with baked beans.

CALF'S LIVER SAUTÉ

Have slices of calf's liver cut very thin. Dredge with flour and sauté in either butter or olive oil, turning and browning quickly. Season with salt and pepper and serve at once. Liver should be slightly rare in the centre for perfection. Allow ½ pound per person.

Variations:

With Bacon: Sauté 3 slices of bacon per person until crisp; drain; serve with sautéed liver.

Pungent: Sauté 2 or 3 green onions, finely chopped, for a few minutes in butter or olive oil. Sauté the liver quickly and add a generous handful of chopped parsley while liver is cooking.

Deviled: Sauté liver very quickly in butter, remove to a hot plate, and add 1 teaspoon dry mustard and 1 tablespoon Worcestershire sauce to the pan; cook with the butter and seasonings about 2 minutes; pour over liver.

With Onions: Sauté liver quickly; add chopped parsley at the last moment and remove to a hot platter; garnish with sautéed onions or French fried onion rings.

CHARCOAL-BROILED KIDNEYS

- Beef, veal, lamb, and pork kidneys may all be successfully cooked over charcoal. Split the kidneys and remove cores; brush with oil or melted butter or margarine, seasoned, if you wish, with garlic or with bacon drippings. Broil over a medium hot fire, (not too long or they will toughen). The kidneys will take from 5 to 15 minutes to cook, depending on size. They are done when brown on the outside but still juicy pink inside. Slice kidneys and serve with melted butter.
- Kidneys may also be cut in pieces, wrapped in bacon, and charcoal-broiled. In this case it is not necessary to brush them with oil. Cook until bacon is very crisp. Serve with broiled tomatoes or, if desired, as part of a mixed grill with broiled sausage and lamb chops or liver .

CHARCOAL-BROILED LIVER

- Liver is at its best when cooked over charcoal. Use beef, veal, or lamb liver, sliced at least 1 inch thick. Brush well with melted butter, oil, or bacon drippings, Broil over a medium hot fire, allowing the meat to become crisply brown on the outside but not dry in the middle. Serve with bacon and fried onions, or broiled tomatoes, or eggplant.

CHARCOAL BROILED LIVER 'N BACON   Serves 4-6

2 pounds liver
    (cut 1 inch thick)

1 teaspoon monosodium glutamate
8 strips lean bacon

Marinade

½ cup olive or salad oil
⅛ teaspoon pepper

⅛ teaspoon garlic powder
            or
¼ teaspoon onion powder

- Soak liver in a mild salt-water solution (1 teaspoon salt to 2 cups water) 30 minutes. Remove, dry surfaces of liver. Sprinkle each side with monosodium glutamate.
- Take each piece, put a strip of bacon under it and another on top of it, and roll up together, secure with a skewer.
- Mix marinade ingredients in a shallow dish or pan. Place liver in marinade, and refrigerate 2 or 3 hours, turning twice during that time.
- Place liver on grill over medium charcoal fire. Broil on each side, turning only once (approximately 15 minutes total cooking time). *Do not over-cook.*
- The meat should be slightly pink on the inside with a mild brown crust on the outside.

CHARCOAL-BROILED PIGS FEET

- Pigs feet must be boiled before they are grilled. Cook them, whole or split, in water to cover, with salt, an onion, and an herb bouquet. Simmer until tender — from 3 to 4 hours.
- Drain, brush well with softened butter or margarine, then roll in crumbs. Broil until nicely browned on all sides.
- Serve with charcoal-roasted potatoes and with sauerkraut heated in a pot at the back of the grill.

CHICKEN LIVER WITH MUSHROOMS   Serves 6

1¾ pounds chicken livers
¼ pound butter or margarine
⅓ cup finely chopped parsley
½ pound fresh mushrooms, sliced
1 teaspoon rosemary

½ clove garlic, minced fine
salt and pepper
olive oil
flour

- Dust livers lightly with flour, heat oil and drop livers in for 5 minutes. Remove, drain.
- Meanwhile, make a sauce by browning butter, then sautéeing garlic and mushrooms.
- Add the seasoning and the chicken livers and sprinkle with the parsley.

SAUTEED BEEF LIVER   Serves 6

1 egg yolk
2 cups mashed potatoes
¼ cup flour
1 teaspoon salt
¼ teaspoon pepper
1½ pounds sliced beef liver

2 tablespoons vegetable oil
2 onions, sliced
1 green pepper, cut lengthwise into strips
1 tomato, cut into wedges
1 10 ounce can condensed beef broth

- Beat egg yolk into mashed potatoes; spoon into pastry bag fitted with a star tip. Pipe potatoes in a border around edge of a 10 inch, round oven-proof platter or board.
- Bake in 400°F. oven 15 minutes, or until potatoes are golden-brown.
- Meanwhile mix flour, salt and pepper on wax paper. Cut liver into serving-size pieces, coat with flour mixture.
- Sauté liver in hot oil in a large frying pan 4 minutes on each side, or until brown and done as you like liver. Arrange slices, overlapping, inside border of potatoes. Keep hot at lowest oven temperature.
- Sauté onions and pepper strip in same pan, adding more oil if needed, until soft and golden. Stir in tomato; sauté 2 minutes longer. Arrange on top of liver.
- Add broth to pan. Bring to boiling, stirring and scraping to dissolve browned bits. Simmer, uncovered, 2 minutes. Pour over liver. Sprinkle with chopped parsley.

SAUTEED SWEETBREADS   Serves 4

2 pairs sweetbreads	salt and pepper
4 tablespoons butter or margarine	lemon

- Soak sweetbreads in cold water for ½ hour, then simmer in salted water for 20 minutes; cool in cold water, remove membranes, tubes and excess fat.
- Cut in serving pieces.
- Sauté seasoned sweetbreads in butter until nicely browned on each side.

Variations:

With Madeira: Dredge sweetbreads in flour and season with salt and pepper. Sauté in 6 tablespoons butter until lightly browned. Add ¼ cup Madeira to pan and cook 1 or 2 minutes. Serve at once on fried toast.

With White Wine: Sauté sweetbreads as above. Add 1 tablespoon chopped parsley and ¼ cup dry white wine to the pan. Serve on a slice of grilled ham.

With Bacon: Sauté bacon strips, (allowing 2 or 3 to a person), until crisp. Sauté the sweetbreads in 2 tablespoons bacon fat and 2 tablespoons butter. Salt and pepper to taste and serve the sweetbreads with the bacon.

SWISS LIVER
Serves 5

1½ pounds calves' liver or beef liver
2 tablespoons butter or margarine
1 tablespoon finely chopped onion
1 tablespoon white wine, preferably chablis

salt and pepper
1 teaspoon freshly chopped parsley

- Pour boiling water over the meat, and let stand 1 minute.
- Drain and cut liver into thin strips about 2 inches long.
- Sauté meat in half of the butter over high heat for about 2 minutes.
- Add onion and sauté another minute.
- Pour wine over the meat.
- Light with a match, let flame briefly. Add the remaining butter, sprinkle with salt, pepper and parsley.

SWEETBREADS AU GRATIN
Serves 6

3 pairs parboiled calf's sweetbreads, thinly sliced
3 tablespoons butter
¼ pound mushrooms, sliced
1 clove garlic, minced
2 teaspoons flour

¾ cup chicken broth
½ teaspoon salt
½ teaspoon black pepper
½ cup sour cream
½ cup grated Parmesan cheese

- Sauté sweetbreads in butter; remove and keep warm.
- Sauté mushrooms 3 minutes; blend in garlic and flour; add broth, stirring steadily, to boiling point; mix in salt, pepper and sour cream.
- Return the sweetbreads, cover and cook over low heat for 15 minutes; top with grated cheese.

SKEWERED CHICKEN LIVERS
Serves 6

18 chicken livers
6 slices bacon
salt and pepper
mushrooms
olive oil

bread crumbs
butter, melted
lemon juice
parsley

- Season chicken livers with pinch of salt and pepper; cut, broil bacon slices, one minute to each side and cut each slice into 6 pieces.
- Take 6 skewers, run one through centre of liver slice, then a mushroom, then a piece of bacon; repeat until all skewers are filled.
- Roll in olive oil, dip in fresh bread crumbs and broil over coals.
- Arrange on a hot dish and pour nectar of melted butter, lemon juice and chopped parsley.

SOUPS AND STEWS AND OTHER MEALS IN A POT

Slow simmered soups and stews are two good ways to expand a menu and still keep food costs and waistlines under control.

They are easy to prepare from scratch or with some convenience type foods. All provide full value in flavour, nutrition and number of servings.

Any of the less tender, less costly cuts of beef, veal, lamb or boiling fowl may be stewed, either cubed, cut in serving pieces or left in one piece. Generally more liquid is used in stewing than for braising or pot-roasting as the pleasures of a good stew depend on a fair amount of flavourful gravy. Often chunky or whole vegetables are cooked along with the meat—added during the last stages of cooking. Beef stew is usually a brown stew; lamb and veal stews are frequently the "light" type, sometimes achieved without pre-browning of the meat. Follow recipe directions.

⇒ BEEF SECTION ⇐

BAKED OXTAIL RAGOUT   Serves 6

4 pounds oxtails
½ cup flour
¾ teaspoon salt
1 teaspoon leaf savory,
   crumbled or equivalent
½ teaspoon pepper

3 tablespoons vegetable oil
1 cup chopped onion
1½ cups vegetable juice
1½ cups water
½ cup dry red wine
1 bay leaf

- Cut oxtails into uniform length pieces.
- Shake to coat well in a mixture of flour, salt, savory and pepper; reserve remaining seasoned flour.
- Brown pieces slowly, part at a time, in oil in a large frying pan; remove to a 2 quart casserole.
- Stir onion into drippings; sauté until soft.
- Stir in reserved seasoned flour; cook, stirring, just until bubbly.
- Stir in vegetable juice, water and wine; continue cooking and stir, until gravy thickens and bubbles 1 minute. Pour over meat in casserole; add bay leaf; cover.
- Bake in 375°F. oven 2 hours, or until meat separates easily from bones.
- Serve with French bread.

BRAISED SHORT RIBS   Serves 6

3 pounds short ribs, cut in
   2 inch serving pieces
3 tablespoons fat
1 teaspoon salt

⅛ teaspoon pepper
3 tablespoons flour
½ cup chopped onion
3 cups tomato juice

- Brown meat in fat about 10 minutes; add salt and pepper; sprinkle browned meat with flour and brown again slightly.
- Add onion and tomato juice, stir well; cover and cook slowly on stove or in 325°F oven 2 - 2¼ hours.

CHILI BEEF STEW

Serves 8

4 pounds beef short ribs
1 cup chopped onion
1 green pepper, halved, seeded and diced
1 clove garlic, chopped
2 tablespoons chili powder
1 16 ounce can tomatoes
1 cup beef broth
¾ teaspoon salt
2 tablespoons flour
¼ cup water
2 16 ounce cans kidney beans, drained
2 cups whole kernel corn, drained

- Heat heavy kettle or Dutch oven; rub fat edges of short ribs over bottom until about 2 tablespoons of fat melt. Brown short ribs well on all sides; remove. Drain off fat.

- Sauté onion, green pepper and garlic in same pan. Stir in chili powder; cook stirring constantly, about 2 minutes.

- Add tomatoes and beef broth. Return ribs to pan. Bring to boiling; lower heat; cover; simmer 2 hours, or until meat is very tender and falls away from the bones.

- Remove meat to serving bowl; keep warm. Carefully remove bones and skim fat from sauce in pan.

- Blend flour and water in a cup; stir into sauce. Cook, stirring constantly, until sauce bubbles and thickens.

- Add kidney beans and corn; heat about 5 minutes. Spoon over meat in serving dish.

BEEF STROGANOFF

Serves 4 - 6

2 pounds round steak, cut ½ inch thick and pounded lightly
3 tablespoons butter or margarine
½ cup minced onion
½ pound mushrooms, sliced
1¼ teaspoons salt
¼ teaspoon black pepper
1 clove garlic, minced
1 teaspoon Worcestershire sauce
4 tablespoons tomato sauce
2 cups sour cream

- Cut steak into strips 1½ inches long by ¼ inch wide.
- Melt butter in frying pan; sauté the onions 5 minutes; add meat and brown.
- Mix in mushrooms, salt, pepper, garlic, Worcestershire sauce and tomato sauce; cover and cook over low heat 30 minutes or until meat is tender.
- Before serving mix in the sour cream; heat, do not boil.
- Serve with rice or noodles.

GERMAN STYLE BEEF STEW   Serves 6

1½ pounds chuck beef, cut in   6 onions, peeled
   1½ inch cubes   6 carrots, scraped and diced
1½ cups frozen peas   2 cups diced turnips
 2 cups tomatoes   salt and pepper

- Cook beef, carrots, onions and tomatoes slowly about 1 hour.
- Add the turnips, peas, (and some water if necessary) for the desired consistency. Add salt and pepper.

Dumplings
1 cup flour   ½ cup milk
1 egg

- Mix and knead ingredients into dough. Twenty minutes before serving drop by spoonfuls into the stew, cover tightly. Steam 20 minutes.

HAMBURGER SKILLET DINNER WITH CORN   Serves 4 - 5

1 pound ground beef   2 tablespoons butter or margarine
1 cup soft bread crumbs   1½ cups whole-kernel corn, drained
1 teaspoon salt   1 medium onion, sliced
⅛ teaspoon pepper   2 cups canned tomatoes, drained

- Mix meat, crumbs, salt and pepper.
- Melt margarine in covered pan, cook meat mixture, stirring frequently, until well browned.
- Add corn, onion and tomatoes; cover and simmer about 25 minutes; Serve in pan.

Variations:

WITH ZUCCHINI
- Brown 1 cup mushrooms with meat.
- Substitute corn with 2 medium zucchini, thinly sliced.
- Add a little garlic powder and hot pepper for extra flavour.

CREAMED WITH CABBAGE
- Brown 1 diced onion with meat.
- Add 4 cups coarsely chopped cabbage, paprika and celery seed.
- Substitute tomatoes with milk.

MEAT BALL SOUP

Serves 4

Meat Balls
½ pound lean chopped beef
1 egg   salt and pepper
Soup
3 carrots, scraped and chopped   2 potatoes, peeled, diced
3 onions, diced   salt and pepper
1 bunch parsley, chopped   ¼ cup canned tomatoes

- Mix meat with egg and seasoning, shape into tiny balls.
- Simmer vegetables together in a pan with 6 cups water for 45 minutes.
- Cook the meat balls a few at a time in the liquid for about 3 minutes.
- Remove and start another batch. When the meat balls are done, transfer to warmed soup plates. Each plate should have 4-5 meat balls.
- Add the canned tomatoes to the soup, heat and pour into the plates.

OLD-FASHIONED BEEF'N VEGETABLE SOUP

Serves 8

6 cups beef broth   1 teaspoon salt
2 potatoes, peeled and diced   ¼ teaspoon pepper
2 carrots, pared and sliced   ½ head green cabbage,
1¼ cup sliced celery   shredded (2 cups)
2 small onions, peeled and   1 cup frozen kernel corn
    quartered   3 cups diced cooked beef
16 ounce can whole tomatoes   1 tablespoon chopped parsley

- Heat beef broth to boiling; add potatoes, carrots, celery, onions, tomatoes, salt and pepper; heat to boiling again; cover; simmer 20 minutes.
- Stir in cabbage, corn and meat; simmer 10 minutes longer or until all vegetables are crisply tender. Sprinkle with parsley. Serve hot.

ONION SOUP

Serves 6

4 large onions, sliced   ¼ teaspoon pepper
3 tablespoons butter or margarine   6 slices French bread, toasted
6 cups beef broth   ½ cup grated Parmesan cheese
1 teaspoon salt   ⅓ cup Gruyère or Swiss cheese

- Sauté onion in butter 15 minutes, or until lightly browned. Stir in beef broth, salt and pepper. Bring to boiling; reduce heat; cover; simmer 30 minutes.
- Ladle soup into 6 ovenproof soup bowls or 12 ounce custard cups, or an 8 cup casserole. Place bread slices on top, sprinkle with cheese.
- Heat in 425°F. oven 10 minutes, then under broiler until top is bubbly and lightly browned.

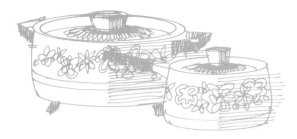

SAVORY OXTAIL SOUP SUPPER   Serves 6

3 pounds oxtails, cut up
2 teaspoons salt
⅛ teaspoon pepper
1 large onion, chopped
2 carrots, pared and sliced
1 cup sliced turnip

2 tablespoons brandy
6 cups water
½ teaspoon leaf savory, crumbled
1 bay leaf
chopped parsley
Eggs Mimosa (recipe follows)

- Spread oxtails in a single layer in shallow roasting pan. Season with salt and pepper; roast in 450°F. oven 45 minutes or until browned; drain off fat, reserving 2 tablespoons.
- Sauté onion, carrots, parsnip and turnip in reserved fat until soft; add browned oxtails.
- Drizzle brandy over, ignite carefully with a lighted match.
- Add water to roasting pan in which oxtails were browned, heat, stirring constantly to dissolve browned bits; pour over oxtails and vegetables in Dutch oven; add savory and bay leaf; bring to boiling, reduce heat, cover, simmer slowly 2 hours or until meat separates easily from bones.
- Ladle into soup bowl; place a half egg in each, sprinkle with parsley.
- Serve with crusty French bread.

EGGS MIMOSA — Cut 3 hard-cooked eggs in half lengthwise. Carefully remove yolks, keeping whites whole. Press yolks through a sieve, spoon back into whites.

SEASONED SHORT RIBS OF BEEF 'N' VEGETABLES   Serves 6

4 pounds short ribs
  salt and pepper
4 tablespoons fat
1 clove garlic
8 small peeled onions
4 carrots, scraped and halved

bay leaf
thyme
water or stock
flour
butter or margarine
chopped parsley

- Cut ribs into serving pieces; season with salt and pepper; brown very quickly in a large frying pan or Dutch oven in hot fat with garlic.
- Add onions, carrots, a bay leaf and just a pinch of thyme, 1 cup liquid; cover and simmer on top of stove or cook in a 325°F. oven approximately 2 hours. (Potatoes may be cooked along with the short ribs.)
- To thicken sauce, add balls of well-blended flour and butter to the liquid just a few minutes before serving.
- Sprinkle with chopped parsley and pass the sauce separately.

SEASONED BEEF STEW

Serves 6-8

2 pounds beef chuck or round,
  cut in 1 x 3-inch strips
2 tablespoons shortening
3 medium onions, coarsely chopped
2 teaspoons ground marjoram
  salt and pepper

2 cups tomato juice
1½ cups dry white wine or bouillon
½ pound lean bacon, cut into strips
2 cups par-boiled whole onions,
  potatoes
¼ cup sliced olives

- Cook onion in hot fat until soft and golden.
- Add meat, sprinkle with marjoram and season to taste with salt and pepper.
- Add juice and wine; simmer for 45 minutes covered, over low heat.
- Partially cook bacon, drain, add to meat with vegetables, continue to simmer, covered for 45 minutes or until meat is tender.
- Remove from heat and stir in olives; serve immediately.

VEGETABLES AND SHORT RIBS

Serves 4

3 to 4 pounds beef short ribs
  salt and pepper
1 onion, sliced
1 cup tomato juice
8 small white onions, peeled

4 medium potatoes, halved
  and peeled
8 carrots, sliced
¾ pound whole green beans

- Brown ribs slowly on all sides; pour off fat and season with salt and pepper.
- Add sliced onion and juice; cover and simmer for 2 hours or until tender.
- Add whole onions and potatoes; cover and simmer for 30 minutes, basting several times with liquid in pan.
- Add carrots and beans, cover and simmer until meat and vegetables are tender.

⫷VEAL SECTION⫸

VEAL STEW   Serves 6

2 pounds veal, cut up for stew
2 lemon wedges
  flour, pepper
2 tablespoons butter or margarine
¼ pound small button mushrooms
8 small onions

1 16 ounce can tiny potatoes, drained
1 cup dry white wine
  (½ cup at a time)
¼ cup chopped fresh parsley
¾ teaspoon celery flakes
  salt

- Lightly flour and pepper veal.
- Brown in butter and squeeze in the lemon juice. Brown the mushrooms and small onions in butter, separately.
- Add half a cup wine first, cover, simmer.
- Brown the potatoes in the same pan, add to the veal, add rest of the wine, parsley, and celery flakes.
- Just before serving, add salt, to taste.

CURRIED LAMB OR VEAL   Serves 6

2 pounds, boneless stewing lamb
  or veal, cubed
1 cup finely chopped onion
2 to 3 tablespoons fat
2 teaspoons salt
⅛ teaspoon pepper
1 cup hot water
1 tablespoon chopped parsley

¼ teaspoon thyme
1 clove garlic, minced
2 tablespoons cornstarch
1 tablespoon curry powder
¼ cup cold water
¼ cup raisins
3 tablespoons chutney, optional
1½ cups chopped, tart apples

- Brown meat and onion in fat, drain, sprinkle with salt and pepper.
- Add hot water, parsley, thyme and garlic; cover and simmer 1 hour until tender.
- Combine cornstarch and curry powder with the cold water to make a smooth paste; blend with some of the hot cooking liquid and add gradually to the meat mixture; stir well.
- Add raisins, chutney and apples; cook 15 minutes longer.
- Serve with cooked rice or noodles.

FRICASSEE OF VEAL

Serves 4

3 cups water
1 carrot
1 onion
1 bay leaf
  sprig parsley
1 stalk celery
¾ teaspoon salt
¼ teaspoon black pepper
2 pounds boneless lean veal,
  cut into 1½ inch cubes

2 tablespoons butter or margarine
¾ cup chopped onion
1 tablespoon flour
½ cup dry white wine
12 small white onions
½ pound mushrooms, sliced
2 egg yolks
½ cup cream
  finely chopped parsley and chives

- Combine first 8 ingredients; bring to a boil and cook over medium heat for 20 minutes.
- Add veal and cook 5 minutes; remove meat; strain and reserve stock.
- Cook onions in melted butter, do not brown; add veal; stir in flour, wine and reserved stock.
- Cover and simmer ½ hour.
- Add onions and mushrooms; cook 30 minutes longer.
- Beat egg yolks and cream; add a little hot sauce to egg-cream mixture; stirring to prevent curdling; return to balance of sauce.
- Reheat but do not boil; sprinkle with chopped parsley and chives.

VEAL SAUTE

Serves 6

2 pounds stewing veal, cut into
  1½ inch cubes
  flour
¼ cup olive oil or salad oil
3 tablespoons butter
3 green onions, finely chopped

1 cup dry white wine
½ cup stock or bouillon
12 white onions, small, peeled
6 to 8 small carrots, scraped
½ pound mushrooms, sliced
  parsley, coarsely chopped

- Dredge veal in seasoned flour; brown quickly in hot oil; reduce heat and add chopped onions, wine and stock.
- Bring to boil and reduce heat to simmering; add white onions and carrots; cover and cook for about 45 minutes.
- Add sliced mushrooms and continue simmering until meat is tender; add parsley.
- Remove meat and vegetables to serving dish; pour sauce over all.

BRAISED VEAL

2 pounds boneless veal
  (shank, breast, neck, flank)
1 cup sliced onion
1 cup sliced carrots

4½ cups tomato juice
2 tablespoons Worcestershire sauce
2 tablespoons chopped parsley

- Cut meat in serving-size pieces; brown well on all sides in a small amount of fat, about 10 minutes.
- Season with salt and pepper, add rest of ingredients; cover and cook slowly in 325°F. oven 1½ to 1¾ hours; uncover for last 15 minutes of cooking.

PORK SECTION

ALSATIAN PORK STEW
Serves 6

2 pounds shoulder pork, cut in
   1 inch cubes
2 tablespoons butter or margarine
1 cup chopped onion
1 tablespoon paprika
1 can condensed chicken broth
¾ cup water
1 teaspoon caraway seeds

1 teaspoon salt
   dash of pepper
1 28 ounce can sauerkraut
2 tablespoons flour
¼ cup water
1 cup dairy sour cream
   chopped parsley

- Brown pork in butter in a heavy kettle or Dutch oven, remove.
- Sauté onion until golden, about 5 minutes; add more butter if needed.
- Stir in paprika; cook 1 minute longer. Return meat.
- Stir in chicken broth, 1 cup water, caraway seeds, salt and pepper.
- Heat to boiling, cover. Simmer 1 hour and 15 minutes.
- Drain and rinse sauerkraut; stir into stew. Simmer 30 minutes longer, or until tender.
- Blend flour and ½ cup water in a small cup; stir into simmering stew. Cook and stir until gravy thickens and boils.
- Lower heat; stir in sour cream, a tablespoon at a time, to prevent curdling. Heat only until heated through. Do not boil. Sprinkle with parsley.

CREOLE SAUSAGE STEW
Serves 4

1 pound pork sausage, cooked
1 cup chopped onion
½ cup chopped green pepper
2 tablespoons flour
4 cups canned tomatoes
2 cups cooked or canned

   whole-kernel corn
1 bay leaf
½ teaspoon thyme
1¼ teaspoons salt
   dash tabasco sauce

- Cut each sausage crosswise into 4 pieces.
- To 2 tablespoons of fat from sausages, sauté onion and pepper for 5 minutes; blend in flour.
- Add tomatoes, corn, bay leaf, thyme, salt and tabasco; cook over low heat 20 minutes.
- Return the sausages and cook 5 minutes longer.

PORK WITH HOT PEPPERS   Serves 6

10 fresh red or green, long hot
   peppers
½ pound lean pork
2 teaspoons soy sauce
2 teaspoons cornstarch
1 teaspoon sugar

1 tablespoon dry sherry
¼ teaspoon monosodium glutamate
   salt to taste
2 tablespoons peanut, vegetable or
   corn oil
¾ cup bamboo shoots, finely shredded

- Core peppers, remove the seeds; cut into fine shreds or 2 inch pieces.
- Place pork on flat surface, using a sharp knife cut into very thin slices.
- Cut slices into very fine shreds (approx. 1 cup); place into mixing bowl, add soy sauce and cornstarch; blend thoroughly.
- Combine sugar, monosodium glutamate and salt, set aside.
- Heat oil in frying pan, when hot add pork mixture.
- Stir-fry to separate shreds, about 3 minutes.
- Add bamboo shoots and sugar mixture, stir-fry 30 seconds.
- Add peppers and cook, stir-fry 1 minute longer.
- Add wine, stir-fry about 15 seconds.
- Serve hot.

⊰LAMB SECTION⊱

ATHENIAN LAMB STEW   Serves 8

2½ pounds lamb shoulder meat,
    cubed
¼ cup vegetable oil
3 medium size onions, chopped
1 clove garlic, minced
4 cups canned tomatoes
8 ounce can tomato sauce

1 cup water
½ teaspoon marjoram
½ teaspoon pepper
1 small eggplant, peeled, cubed
1 large green pepper, seeded, cubed
3 cups uncooked elbow macaroni

- Brown meat lightly in oil in a Dutch Oven.
- Remove, add garlic and onions; sauté 5 minutes or until soft.
- Add lamb cubes, tomatoes, tomato sauce, water, salt, marjoram and pepper; bring to boiling, lower heat and simmer, covered 1 hour.
- Add eggplant, green pepper and macaroni, cook 30 minutes longer or until meat and macaroni are tender.

IRISH STEW

Serves 8

3 pounds shoulder of lamb, cut in
   1½ inch cubes, browned
2 pounds potatoes, peeled and
   sliced ½ inch thick
2 cups sliced onion
2 teaspoons salt

½ teaspoon white pepper
½ teaspoon thyme
1 bay leaf
3 sprigs parsley
1 stalk celery
1½ cups water

- Arrange successive layers of meat, potatoes and onions in casserole; sprinkle each layer with salt, pepper and thyme.
- Add bay leaf, parsley, celery and water; cover and simmer 2 to 3 hours.

Variations:

VEGETABLE IRISH STEW
- Add 8 carrots, peeled and sliced and ½ cabbage, shredded.

MIDDLE EAST LAMB STEW
- Omit potatoes and celery; add 1 clove garlic, minced and ½ teaspoon coriander.
- Half hour before serving stir in 3 cups deep browned beans with pork and tomato sauce.

EASTERN LAMB STEW
- Omit potatoes and celery and water.
- Add ¼ teaspoon cinnamon, ¼ teaspoon nutmeg, ⅛ teaspoon allspice and 3½ cups chicken broth.
- During last hour of cooking add 1 cup uncooked rice and 1 pound prunes, pre-soaked.

FRENCH LAMB STEW
- Omit potatoes and celery.
- Add to meat, 2 tablespoons flour, 1 tablespoon tomato paste and 2 garlic cloves, minced.
- During last 30 minutes of cooking add 4 cups lima beans.

CREOLE LAMB STEW
- Omit potatoes and celery.
- Marinate lamb overnight in onions, salt, pepper, bay leaf, 2 cups dry red wine, 1 cup sliced green pepper, 2 cloves garlic, minced and 6 peppercorns.
- Brown meat and 3 slices salt pork, diced.
- Add marinade and 1 cup diced tomatoes; cover and bake in 300°F. oven for 3 hours; serve with parsley.

ISLAND LAMB CURRY

Serves 8

3 pounds boneless lamb,
cut in 1 inch cubes
2 tablespoons butter or margarine
¾ cup finely chopped onion
1 teaspoon salt
2 tablespoons curry powder

¼ cup chopped preserved ginger
1½ cups beef broth
2 tablespoons lime or lemon juice
½ cup packaged finely grated coconut
1 cup light cream

- Brown onions and lamb in butter; stir in salt and curry powder; cook 2 minutes.
- Add ginger and broth; cover and cook over low heat 1 hour.
- Stir lime or lemon juice into the pan juices, then add coconut and cream; cook 10 minutes but do not let boil.
- Serve with rice.

LAMB AND BEAN STEW

Serves 6

1½ pounds stewing lamb, cubed
1¼ cups sliced onions
2 tablespoons butter or margarine
2 cups beef bouillon
1½ cups diced raw potatoes
2 cups frozen green beans
2 green peppers, chopped,
seeds removed

1 small can water chestnuts, sliced
salt and pepper
2 teaspoons Worcestershire sauce
2 tablespoons butter and flour
(2 tablespoons of each, mixed together)

- Brown the lamb and onions in butter.
- Add the bouillon and simmer 1½ hours or until the meat is almost tender.
- Add potatoes, green beans, green peppers, water chestnuts, salt, pepper and Worcestershire sauce.
- Cook 25 minutes or until vegetables are tender crisp. Add butter and flour mixture, cook 5 minutes longer, stir constantly.

SPICY SHOULDER OF LAMB

Serves 6 - 8

4 pounds shoulder of lamb,
cut in 6-8 pieces
½ cup chili sauce
¼ cup wine vinegar
½ cup water
½ cup thinly sliced onion

1 clove garlic, minced
1 teaspoon salt
1½ teaspoons chili powder
⅛ teaspoon tabasco
1 tablespoon Worcestershire sauce
½ teaspoon garlic powder

- Brown lamb in a Dutch oven or heavy saucepan; pour off the fat.
- Blend remaining ingredients; add to lamb; cover and bake in 350°F. oven 1½ hours; uncover for the last 15 minutes.

⇒ POULTRY SECTION ⇐

CHICKEN FRICASSEE, CANADIAN-STYLE   Serves 4 - 6

4 to 5 pounds chicken, disjointed	2 tablespoons butter or margarine
1 onion	2 tablespoons flour
2 cloves	1 cup cream
1 bay leaf	2 egg yolks
parsley	lemon juice
2 teaspoons salt	

- Place chicken parts in a large kettle with onion stuck with cloves, bay leaf and parsley.
- Cover with cold water, bring to boiling point, cover and simmer 1 hour.
- Add ½ teaspoon salt per pound of chicken and continue simmering until the chicken is tender but not mushy.
- Remove chicken from broth and place in a casserole, keep warm.
- Skim off fat and strain the broth.
- Melt butter, add flour, blend well over low heat to a thick paste; gradually add 2 cups of chicken broth, stirring constantly, to thicken slightly.
- Add cream mixed with egg yolks; stirring constantly until thoroughly blended, do not allow to boil.
- Add a generous sprinkling of chopped parsley and a squeeze of lemon juice.
- Arrange chicken on a platter, surround with mounds of boiled rice or buttered noodles and cover with sauce; sprinkle additional parsley on top.

Variations:

CHICKEN PAPRIKA

- Add 2 or more teaspoons paprika to the butter-and-flour mixture when making sauce.
- Proceed as above, but omit the chopped parsley; sprinkle paprika on top when serving.

WITH CORN BREAD

- When chicken is removed from the broth, cut meat from the bones in large sections for serving.
- Prepare sauce and add to it the chicken pieces and 12 mushroom caps which have been sautéed in butter.
- Blend well and serve over thin squares of hot corn bread, or serve with spoon bread.

CHICKEN PIE

- Place pieces of chicken in a 2-quart casserole with 12 sautéed mushroom caps and top with a rich biscuit dough.

CHICKEN IN A POT

Serves 8

2 frying chicken, about 2½ pounds
  each, cut in quarters
½ cup olive or salad oil
1 large onion, chopped
1 clove garlic, minced

1 teaspoon salt
¾ teaspoon pepper
½ cup drained canned tomatoes
½ cup dry white wine

- In Dutch oven or heavy pot, brown chicken in olive oil until golden.
- Sprinkle with onion, garlic, salt and pepper; cover and simmer for 30 minutes.
- Add tomato and wine; simmer for 30 minutes longer or until chicken is tender.

CHICKEN, LAMB & RICE STEW

Serves 8

2 cups chopped onions
2 tablespoons olive oil
1 broiler-fryer chicken, cut-up
1 pound lean lamb, cut into
  1½ inch cubes
3 cups water
4 carrots, pared and cut into
  1 inch pieces
2 teaspoons salt
½ teaspoon pepper
¼ teaspoon ground ginger

1 three inch piece stick cinnamon
1 teaspoon salt
1 cup water
2¾ cups rice
4 small zucchini, washed and cut
  into ½ inch slices
2 tomatoes, chopped
20 ounce can chick peas, drained
1 cup seedless raisins
3 tablespoons butter or margarine,
  melted

- Sauté onions until golden in oil. Transfer to a stock pot or similar deep narrow kettle. Brown chicken and lamb in same frying pan; transfer to stock pot.
- Add water to pan; bring to boiling, scraping off brown bits; pour over meat.
- Stir in carrots, salt, pepper, ginger and cinnamon; bring to boiling.
- Meanwhile, cook rice according to package directions. Toss with melted butter.
- Stir zucchini, tomatoes, peas and raisins into stew. Simmer 30 minutes longer, or until meats and vegetables are tender.
- Thicken stew with a little flour mixed with water.
- To serve, spoon stew into centre of a deep platter. Arrange the steamed buttered rice around edge.

CHICKEN LIMA STEW   Serves 6

1 pound dried baby lima beans	1 cup coarsely chopped carrot
6 cups water	1 teaspoon paprika
2½ pound chicken, cut up	1 teaspoon salt
2 tablespoons vegetable oil	¼ teaspoon pepper
1 clove garlic, chopped	1 bay leaf
1 large onion, chopped	
1 green pepper, seeded, coarsely chopped	

- Pick over and wash limas. Put limas and water in a heavy kettle.
- Bring to boiling; remove from heat. Let stand 1 hour.
- Wash and dry chicken. Heat oil in a frying pan. Add chicken pieces and brown well. Remove.
- Drain off all but 1 tablespoon of fat from pan; add garlic, onion, green pepper and carrot, cook 2 minutes, stirring constantly.
- Add browned chicken, sautéed vegetables, salt, pepper and bay leaf to lima. Cover; bring to boiling; simmer 1 hour, or until chicken is tender.

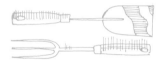

CHICKEN'N MEATBALL STEW   Serves 6

1½ pounds chicken wings	½ pound ground beef
1 onion, chopped	3 cups canned or cooked mixed vegetables
5 cups water	1 small head cabbage, shredded
2 cups stewed tomatoes	2 cups instant mashed potato flakes
2 tablespoons bottled steak sauce	¼ cup chopped parsley
⅛ teaspoon cayenne	
3 teaspoons salt	

- Cut apart chicken wings at joints. Combine with onion, water, tomatoes, steak sauce, cayenne and 2 teaspoons of the salt in a large heavy kettle or Dutch oven.
- Heat to boiling; lower heat; cover. Simmer 30 minutes.
- Mix ground beef lightly with remaining salt; shape into 18 little meatballs.
- Add mixed vegetables and cabbage to chicken mixture; bring to a boil; add meatballs; lower heat; cover. Simmer 10 minutes. Stir in potato flakes. Remove from heat.
- Sprinkle with parsley. Spoon into soup bowls.

MULLIGATAWNY SOUP Serves 6

3 medium carrots, pared and sliced
2 stalks of celery, sliced
6 cups chicken broth
3 cups cooked diced chicken
1 cup chopped onion
3 tablespoons butter or margarine
1 apple, pared, quartered, cored and chopped

2 tablespoons curry powder
¾ teaspoon salt
¼ cup flour
1 tablespoon lemon juice
2 cups hot cooked rice
¼ cup chopped parsley
6 lemon slices

- Cook carrots and celery in 1 cup broth 20 minutes, or until tender.
- Add chicken; heat until hot; cover; keep warm.
- Sauté onion until soft in butter in Dutch oven; stir in apple, curry powder and salt; sauté 5 minutes longer, or until apple is soft; add flour.
- Gradually stir in remaining chicken broth; heat to boiling, stir constantly; reduce heat; cover; simmer 15 minutes.
- Add vegetables and chicken with the broth they were cooked in; bring just to boiling. Stir in lemon juice.
- Ladle into soup plates or bowls; pass hot cooked rice, chopped parsley and lemon slices. Serve with French bread.

SKILLET TOMATO CHICKEN Serves 4 - 6

1 3 or 3½ pound chicken, cut up
½ cup onion slices
1 clove garlic, minced
2 tablespoons flour

1 teaspoon salt
2 cups tomatoes
1 cup sour cream
½ cup grated Parmesan cheese

- Brown chicken lightly in ¼-inch hot fat; remove; drain, reserving 2 tablespoons drippings.
- Cook onion and garlic in drippings until tender; blend in flour, salt and tomatoes; mix well.
- Add chicken; cover, cook slowly about 40 minutes; remove chicken; add sour cream and Parmesan; stir over low heat just till hot; pour over chicken.

TASTY CHICKEN STEW Serves 6

2½-3 lbs chicken cut up
2 tablespoons butter or margarine
.1 cup long grain rice
4 cups chicken broth
4 ounce can pimientos, cut in large pieces

10 ounce package frozen asparagus spears
12 ounce package frozen peas
¾ cup green olives, pitted or stuffed
salt, pepper

- Sauté chicken until browned on both sides, transfer to a deep casserole.
- Add rice, broth, pimientos, asparagus, peas and olives.
- Cover, cook over low heat 45 minutes, or until tender. All salt and pepper as needed.

TURKEY STEW

- Allow ½ to ¾ pound per serving of breast, legs, wings and/or necks. Half cover turkey pieces with water. Add desired seasonings (salt, pepper, bay leaf, curry powder, rosemary or oregano etc.) a small onion sliced, 1 carrot sliced, some chopped celery leaves or sliced celery.
- Bring to boil, reduce heat and simmer covered 1½ to 2 hours until fork tender. Add additional water if necessary, during cooking.
- Cool enough to strip meat from bones in large pieces. Strain broth and thicken for gravy. Allow 2 tablespoons flour for each cup of gravy and sufficient water or milk to make flour into a paste easily mixed with the hot broth. Add turkey and required vegetables, bring to boil and cook covered 10 minutes, drop dumpling dough on top of meat and vegetables so that it steams rather than stews in the gravy. This makes feather-light rather than heavy or soggy dumplings. Reduce heat slightly so that gravy boils gently, cover pan with close fitting lid, and cook without peaking 15 minutes.

  Note: If medium-sized potatoes are cut into pieces or quarters, carrots left whole, or cut in half lengthwise (depending upon size), onions sliced, and turnips cut into ⅓ inch dice, they should cook tender in the 15 minutes.

TURKEY VEGETABLE SOUP   Makes 10 cups

1 turkey carcass (from 20-24 pound turkey)	1 tablespoon salt
	½ teaspoon poultry seasoning
9 cups water	¼ teaspoon pepper
1 19 ounce can tomatoes	½ cup uncooked rice or noodles
¾ cup sliced celery	1 package frozen mixed vegetables
¾ cup chopped onion	

- Break turkey carcass into pieces and place in large kettle.
- Add remaining ingredients except rice or noodles and frozen vegetables.
- Cover and bring to a boil. Reduce heat and simmer approximately 1½ hours.
- Separate meat from bones. Return meat to soup with rice or noodles and mixed vegetables. Cover and continue to simmer until rice or noodles are tender (about 20 minutes).

ALL MEAT STEW   Serves 6

½ pound lean pork, cubed	1 large onion, quartered
1 pound lean beef, cubed	2 teaspoons salt
½ pound lean veal, cubed	1 teaspoon black pepper
½ pound lean lamb, cubed	1 bay leaf

- Place all ingredients in a casserole with enough water to cover.
- Cook 5-6 hours in a 325°F. oven. Serve from casserole.

CASSEROLES, SUPPER DISHES AND COMPANY MEALS

If it combines a protein food like meat, egg, cheese, fish, with other ingredients for flavour, texture and variety, and you cook it in the oven — it's a casserole.

Casseroles are wonderful ways to use a wide variety of foods in combination to have — a meal-in-a-dish.

Meat, cereal, vegetable and often milk with a fruit dessert complete a good nutritional balance. The following ideas are helpful hints when adding variety of casseroles to your menus.

Right from the beginning, whenever you pick up a new cookbook you have company in mind.

After all, a budget that only allows for the same number of people night after night isn't realistic.

The recipes are geared for those occasions when you have at least 8 to feed — economically. Of course, if you are planning a dinner for four or six almost any recipe in this book will fit that occasion.

Larger recipes can be a good safeguard for unexpected guests, second helpings or for leftovers, to store in the freezer for unexpected guests or a late night home.

Although the recipes keep economy in mind, your guests will only be aware that you are a marvelous cook.

SUBSTITUTIONS

When preparing casseroles from leftovers you may run across a necessary ingredient you don't have. The following chart is designed to help you make-do.

IF YOU DON'T HAVE:	SUBSTITUTE THE FOLLOWING:
1 whole egg	2 egg yolks
1 tablespoon flour (for thickening)	½ tablespoon cornstarch or 1 tablespoon granular tapioca or 2 teaspoons quick cooking tapioca or 2 tablespoons of granular cereal
1 cup sifted flour	1 cup unsifted minus 2 tablespoons
1 cup honey	1¼ cups sugar plus ¼ cup liquid
1 cup corn syrup	1 cup sugar plus ¼ cup liquid
1 cup milk	½ cup evaporated milk plus ½ cup water or approximately ¼ cup nonfat dry milk plus water to make 1 cup fluid milk or approximately ⅓ cup instant nonfat dry milk plus water to make 1 cup fluid milk
1 medium-size onion, chopped	1 tablespoon instant minced onion, rehydrated

Careful shopping does pay off. If you save only 5c on each meal, you'll save up to $50 by the end of the year. Casseroles offer an easy way to stretch these savings even further. Following are some tips to help you get started.

1. Use instant nonfat dry milk whenever a casserole calls for a sauce or gravy with a milk base. It's much less expensive than whole milk, and you'll never know the difference!

2. Use tag ends of bread for casserole toppings. Cut sliced bread into tiny cubes or pull apart into crumbs, toss with melted butter or margarine, grated cheese or mixed dry herbs. Then sprinkle on top of your casserole before baking. Another bread idea: slice French bread very thin, butter slices and place, overlapping, around the rim of the casserole.

3. Save bits of dry cereal in a jar, then crush or whirl in a blender for a ready-to-use casserole crumb topper.

4. For a quick casserole that still watches the budget, try the following: Heat canned beans in a casserole then top with: crisp bacon or thin slices of ham or back bacon; a sprinkle of grated Parmesan cheese or finely minced onion; paper-thin green-pepper rings; a drizzle of molasses sparked with mustard; heat-and-serve sausage links or thin pork chops.

5. For a convenience-food casserole, try this: Start with precooked rice or macaroni, or curried, Spanish or Chinese fried-rice mix. Add one of the following — a can of drained flaked tuna, diced canned luncheon meat or cut-up leftover meat from a roast. Add canned tomato sauce and heat all together in the oven.

6. Prepare packaged Spanish-rice mix and place in a baking dish. Arrange canned Vienna sausages on top; sprinkle all generously with grated Cheddar cheese. Bake in a 400°F. oven 20 minutes, or until bubbly hot and cheese melts.

7. Leftover meats and vegetables are naturals for casseroles, and they can cut costs dramatically over purchasing special ingredients.

8. It's a good idea, therefore, to buy foods with leftovers in mind, to use for casseroles.

9. Use up leftover sauces and gravies in casseroles, combined with vegetables and meat.

BEEF SECTION

BEAN BAKE
Serves 6

1 pound dried red kidney beans	1 16 ounce can tomatoes
6 cups water	1½ teaspoon salt
1 large onion, chopped	1 teaspoon marjoram
1 pound ground beef	

- Pick over beans and rinse. Place in a large saucepan, add water. Heat to boiling; boil 2 minutes; remove from heat, cover. Allow to stand 1 hour.
- Add chopped onion to saucepan. Heat to boiling; reduce heat, simmer 1 hour.
- While beans cook, brown ground beef in a large frying pan; break into small pieces. Stir in tomatoes, salt and marjoram; simmer 5 minutes.
- Drain beans, reserving liquid. Combine beans and ground beef mixture in a 2½ quart casserole. Stir in 1 cup of reserved bean liquid. Cover.
- Bake in 325°F. oven 2½ hours; remove cover. Bake 30 minutes longer, or until beans are tender. (Should beans begin to get dry during baking, add some of the reserved bean liquid, just enough to moisten the surface.)

BEEF BURGUNDY   Serves 6-8

3-4 pounds boneless beef chuck, cubed
  flour, salt and pepper
1 10 ounce can tomato soup
2 soup cans Burgundy
1 clove garlic

1 bay leaf
1 onion, chopped
1 carrot, chopped
1 small bunch parsley, finely chopped
1 stalk celery, chopped

- Shake the cubes of beef in a bag with flour, salt and pepper.
- Brown in the bottom of a Dutch oven, using no fat.
- Add the soup, wine, onion, garlic, carrot, parsley, celery, and bay leaf.
- Simmer 2-3 hours until meat is tender and liquid reduced and thickened.
- Remove the celery, bay leaf, and parsley, discard or add to soup (opt.).

BEEFSTEAK AND KIDNEY PIE   Serves 6

3 pounds rump or round steak,
  cut in strips
  flour
  salt and pepper
6 or 8 lamb kidneys, skinned,
  cleaned and sliced thin
  vegetable oil

¼ teaspoon thyme
1 large onion, chopped
  water or stock
3 tablespoons butter or margarine
  pastry dough
1 egg yolk

- Dredge steak with flour and season with salt and pepper.
- Brown beef very quickly in hot fat; add thyme, onion and enough water or stock to just cover the meat; simmer 1 to 1½ hours.
- Brown kidneys very quickly in 3 tablespoons butter.
- Fill a 2-quart casserole with separate layers of meat and kidneys; add the liquid from the cooked beef, letting it come to an inch from the top. It is wise to place a custard cup or jelly glass in the centre of the casserole to hold up the crust.
- Cover the casserole with a rich pastry dough; make several slashes in the pastry and brush with lightly beaten egg yolk.
- Place in a 450°F. oven for 10 minutes, reduce to 350°F. and bake until crust is nicely browned, about ½ hour.
- Serve with plain boiled potatoes and a green salad.

BEEFY CASSEROLE   Serves 6

1 pound ground beef
4 ounces uncooked elbow macaroni
1 can condensed cream
  of mushroom soup
¾ cup milk
⅔ cup catsup

½ cup shredded Cheddar cheese
¼ cup chopped green pepper
  (optional)
4 tablespoons chopped onion
¾ teaspoon salt
½ cup dried bread crumbs

- Cook and stir meat until browned, drain off excess fat.
- Cook macaroni as per package directions, drain.
- In ungreased 2 quart casserole mix all ingredients except bread crumbs.
- Top with bread crumbs, cover and bake in 350°F. oven for 40 minutes.

BUDGET SUKIYAKI   Serves 6

1½ pound boneless chuck steak
¼ cup vegetable oil
2 medium-size potatoes, pared and
  thinly sliced
2 cups green beans, tipped and cut
  in 1 inch pieces
1 green pepper, halved, seeded and
  cut into thin strips
1 sweet red pepper, halved, seeded
  and cut into thin strips

1½ cup thinly sliced celery
½ cup soy sauce
1 cup water
1 small head Chinese cabbage,
  shredded
1 bunch green onion, trimmed and
  cut into 2 inch pieces
4 large mushrooms, trimmed and
  sliced (optional)

- Trim all fat from meat; cut into very thin strips.
- Heat oil in a large frying pan; add steak strips and sauté, 2 to 3 minutes, or until brown; remove and keep warm.
- Add potatoes, green beans, green and red pepper and celery; sauté 2 to 3 minutes, or until vegetables start to soften.
- Combine soy sauce and water in a cup; pour over vegetables; cover. Simmer 5 minutes.
- Stir in shredded cabbage, green onions and mushrooms; cover. Cook 5 minutes longer, or until cabbage wilts and vegetables are crisply tender.
- Return cooked steak strips to pan and heat until piping-hot.
- Serve with hot cooked rice and more soy sauce.

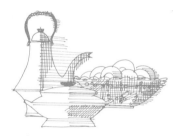

COTTAGE PIE   Serves 4

4 cups mashed potatoes
3 onions, diced
2 tablespoons butter
  cooked vegetables (peas, carrots,
  beans, etc.)

1 pound ground beef
¾ cup beef gravy
2 tablespoons Burgundy

- Butter a pie plate, line the bottom and sides with slightly more than half the mashed potatoes.
- Sauté chopped onion in butter and spread on mashed potatoes.
- Strew cooked vegetables on top.
- Sauté beef, add gravy and wine to meat.
- Put on top of vegetables, top with rest of mashed potatoes.
- Groove the top of the mashed potatoes one way and then criss-cross at 2 inch intervals with the tines of a fork.
- Bake in a 350°F. oven 30 minutes or until brown.

GOURMET CHILI & BEANS AND RICE   Serves 8

2½ pounds round steak or chuck,
    cut in 1½ inch cubes
¼ cup fat from steak, chopped
2 tablespoons olive oil
1 clove garlic, chopped
3 green onions, tops and bottoms,
    chopped

2 cups beef bouillon
¼ cup, chili powder
½ teaspoon cumin
   salt, pepper

- Brown meat and fat in olive oil, add onions and garlic, sprinkle with seasonings, add beef bouillon.
- Bring the mixture to a boil, cover, turn heat down low, and simmer for several hours.
- The exact amount of time doesn't matter. It may be done the day before and allowed to "ripen" in the refrigerator or frozen. (If it is frozen, the seasonings must be checked on reheating and some fresh chili powder and freshly chopped onion added before reheating.)

GREEK STYLE CABBAGE ROLLS   Serves 5

1 medium-sized head cabbage
1 pound ground beef
2 onions, chopped
1 cup uncooked washed rice

salt, pepper, oregano
2 eggs, slightly beaten
juice of 1 lemon

- Pull leaves of cabbage apart, drop in boiling water 1 minute, to make pliable.
- Mix ground beef with onions, raw rice, salt, pepper and oregano.
- Put a spoonful on each leaf (as many as you want to use).
- Roll up, tucking in the ends, and arrange in a medium-sized casserole, layer if necessary.
- Cover with water, bake in 350°F. oven or cook on top of stove over low heat for 30 minutes.
- Remove cover, drain cabbage rolls, reserve liquid.
- Put the slightly beaten eggs and lemon juice in a small saucepan.
- Cook over low heat, adding a little liquid from the cabbage until the sauce is smooth and thickened.
- Pour over the cabbage rolls and serve.

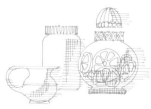

GROUND BEEF AND KIDNEY PIE   Serves 4

1 beef kidney	¼ cup cold water
1 tablespoon shortening	1 teaspoon salt
2 cups boiling water	¼ teaspoon pepper
1 pound ground beef	1 teaspoon steak sauce
1 medium onion, chopped	pastry
2 tablespoons flour	

- Cut kidney into crosswise slices; remove fat and gristle; then cube.
- Rinse in cold water, dry; brown.
- Add boiling water, cover, simmer 1 hour or until tender.
- Cook beef and onion, stirring until meat loses its red colour; add kidney and liquid.
- Blend flour with cold water, stir into mixture; cook and stir until slightly thickened.
- Add seasonings and pour into 1-quart casserole.
- Roll pastry to ⅛-inch thickness and place over top; cut slits to allow steam to escape.
- Brush with slightly beaten egg white, if desired.
- Bake in 400°F. oven for 20 minutes or until pastry is brown.

HOMEMADE MEAT SAUCE   12 cups sauce

1 large onion, chopped	2 tablespoons sugar
2 cloves garlic, minced	1 tablespoon leaf oregano, crumbled
¼ cup vegetable oil	1 tablespoon leaf basil, crumbled
1 pound ground beef	2 teaspoons salt
2 Italian sausages, chopped	½ teaspoon pepper
8 cups Italian tomatoes	¼ cup grated Parmesan cheese
2 6 ounce cans tomato paste	

- Sauté onion and garlic in oil in a frying pan, until soft; brown beef and sausage. Pour off all but 2 tablespoons fat.
- Stir in all remaining ingredients except cheese. Simmer, uncovered, stirring frequently, 45 minutes or until sauce thickens. Stir in Parmesan cheese; cool.
- Freeze in plastic containers.

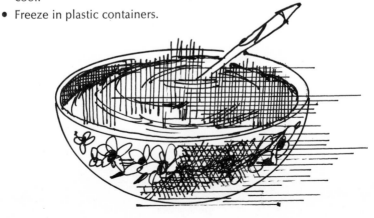

ITALIAN STYLE BEEF ROLLS WITH SPAGHETTI Serves 6

1½ pounds beef chuck, thinly sliced
1 cup cottage cheese (cream style)
1 3 ounce can sliced mushrooms, drained
¼ cup vegetable oil
1 clove garlic
⅔ cup chopped onions
1 16 ounce can tomatoes
1 6 ounce can tomato paste
¼ teaspoon oregano
⅛ teaspoon sage
2 teaspoons salt
1 cup cooked peas
3 quarts boiling water
1 8 ounce package spaghetti

- Combine cheese and mushrooms, spread on meat slices; roll up each slice and secure with string.
- Heat oil in large frying pan; add meat rolls and garlic. Cook until brown.
- Remove rolls, add onions, cook until brown.
- Add next 4 ingredients with ½ salt, mix well.
- Add meat rolls, cover, simmer 1 hour or until meat is tender.
- Add peas, heat thoroughly.
- Add remaining salt to rapidly boiling water, cook spaghetti. Drain.
- Put in serving dish and spoon meat rolls over spaghetti. (Remove string)
- Pour sauce over all.

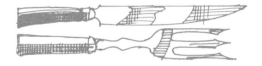

LASAGNE Serves 8

2 medium onions, chopped
2 cloves garlic, chopped
2 tablespoons vegetable oil
1 cup sliced pepperoni OR use ground beef
2 14 ounce cans tomato sauce
1 teaspoon oregano
12 ounces lasagne
8 ounces cottage cheese
2 tablespoons Parmesan cheese, grated
1 egg, beaten
½ teaspoon salt
8 slices Mozzarella cheese

- Sauté onions and garlic in oil. Add pepperoni, tomato sauce and oregano.
- Simmer, uncovered, 20 minutes, stirring occasionally.
- Cook lasagne according to package directions. Drain and rinse under cold water.
- Mix together cottage cheese, Parmesan cheese, beaten egg and salt.
- Pour half of the sauce in a baking dish 9 x 13 inches, and cover with half the lasagne.
- Spread all cottage cheese mixture over the lasagne, then cover with remaining lasagne.
- Pour remaining sauce on top and cover with slices of Mozzarella cheese.
- Bake in 350°F. oven 20 minutes.

LASAGNE WITH MEATBALLS

Serves 8 - 10

¾ pound lean beef, ground
½ teaspoon salt
¼ teaspoon pepper
1 teaspoon grated lemon rind
2 tablespoons olive oil

3 cups tomato sauce
1 pound lasagne cooked, drained
1 pound cottage cheese
1 pound Mozzarella cheese, cubed
1½ cups grated Parmesan cheese

- Mix beef, salt, pepper, and lemon rind; shape into balls the size of a large marble; brown in hot oil.
- Cover bottom of a large 2 inch deep baking dish sparingly with tomato sauce; line with lasagne; dot with half of cheeses; spread with half of remaining sauce; top with meat.
- Cover with remaining lasagne sauce and cheeses.
- Bake in 325°F. oven for 45 minutes; cool slightly.

MIDDLE EAST MEAT CROQUETTES

Serves 6

1 cup white bread cubes
½ cup milk
1 pound ground lean beef
1 pound ground lean lamb
¾ cup finely chopped onion
1 teaspoon salt

¼ teaspoon cayenne pepper
¼ teaspoon crushed cumin seed
3 tablespoons chopped parsley
2 eggs, beaten
½ cup dry bread crumbs
4 tablespoons butter or margarine

- Soak bread in milk for 5 minutes; mash smooth.
- Mix together next 8 ingredients with soaked bread; shape into 12 croquettes.
- Dip in the dry bread crumbs.
- Sauté in melted butter over low heat until browned on both sides, adding more butter as needed.

OLDE ENGLISH CASSEROLE

Serves 6

8 ounces noodles, cooked and drained
1½ pounds ground beef
1 large size onion, thinly sliced
1 tablespoon flour
½ teaspoon seasoned salt

¼ teaspoon lemon pepper
1 3-4 ounce can sliced mushrooms
2 cups cooked green beans, drained
2 cups tomato sauce
1 cup grated Cheddar cheese

- Place cooked noodles in a lightly greased 2 quart casserole.
- Brown beef; remove to a bowl; drain all but 1 tablespoon fat from frying pan.
- Sauté onion in fat until tender; return beef.
- Blend in flour, seasoned salt and lemon pepper; stir in sliced mushrooms and liquid, green beans and tomato sauce.
- Spoon mixture over noodles, spreading evenly; sprinkle with cheese.
- Bake in a 350°F. oven 30 minutes.

ORIENTAL STYLE MEAT BALLS   Serves 6

1 pound ground beef
1 egg beaten
¾ teaspoon salt

⅛ teaspoon pepper
¼ teaspoon ginger

SAUCE:
½ cup chopped onion
¾ cup celery, diagonally sliced
2 tablespoons fat
1 cup beef bouillon
1 tablespoon soy sauce
1½ tablespoons sugar

½ teaspoon ginger
2 tablespoons cornstarch
¼ cup vinegar
1 14 ounce can pineapple tidbits
½ cup syrup from pineapple

- Mix all ingredients for meat balls and shape in 1¼ inch balls.
- Bake in 325°F. oven for 35 minutes.
- To make sauce, sauté onion and celery in fat until onion is transparent.
- Add remaining ingredients except pineapple and meatballs.
- Stir and cook until thick and clear.
- Add pineapple and meat balls. Cover and simmer 10 minutes.
- Serve over rice.

POLYNESIAN SHORT RIBS   Serves 6

3 pounds short ribs of beef
¼ cup flour
2 tablespoons shortening or oil
1 can condensed beef broth
1 cup dried apricots
        OR
½ cup raisins

2 tablespoons brown sugar
2 tablespoons vinegar
¼ teaspoon cinnamon
¼ teaspoon cloves
¼ teaspoon allspice
⅛ teaspoon mace

- Dust ribs with flour, brown on all sides in frying pan in oil; remove excess drippings.
- Combine remaining ingredients and pour over ribs.
- Cook over low heat, covered 2½ hours or until tender.

SHEPHERD'S PIE

Serves 4 - 5

1 pound ground beef
1 egg
2 cups soft bread crumbs
salt and pepper
3 tablespoons butter or margarine
1 large onion, minced
1 tablespoon flour

1 cup undrained mushrooms
2 cups canned tomatoes
10 ounce package frozen
peas and carrots, thawed
⅛ teaspoon ground oregano
2 cups whipped potatoes

- Mix first 4 ingredients; shape into 12 large balls.
- Brown on all sides in 2 tablespoons butter in Dutch oven or large frying pan.
- Remove meatballs and brown onion in drippings; blend in flour, mushrooms and tomatoes; add meatballs, bring to boil.
- Cover, simmer for 30 minutes; add peas and carrots and bring to boil; add oregano and season to taste.
- Pour into shallow 2-quart baking dish; spread whipped potatoes on top of meat mixture; put under broiler until lightly browned.

SPINACH LASAGNA

Serves 12

1 pound ground beef
½ pound sweet Italian sausages
2 cups chopped onions
1 clove of garlic, minced
4 cups Italian tomatoes with juice
2 teaspoons salt
2 teaspoons Italian herbs, crumbled
½ teaspoon pepper

1 pound lasagna noodles
2 eggs
2 10 ounce packages frozen chopped
spinach, thawed, drained
1 pound cottage cheese
1 cup grated Parmesan cheese
2 6 ounce packages sliced
Mozzarella cheese

- Brown ground beef and Italian sausages in a large kettle; reserve.
- Pour off all but 3 tablespoons of the fat. Sauté onion and garlic until soft in fat.
- Return meat to kettle with tomatoes, ½ teaspoon salt, Italian herbs and pepper. Simmer over low heat, stirring occasionally 30 minutes.
- Cook lasagna noodles; drain and place in a bowl of cold water to keep separated.
- Beat eggs in a large bowl; add spinach, cottage cheese and remaining salt.
- When ready to assemble: Drain noodles on paper toweling; arrange 3 strips on the bottom of each of two 13x9x2-inch baking dishes.
- Spoon part of the cheese-spinach mixture over noodles; add part of meat sauce; sprinkle with grated Parmesan cheese.
- Continue layering until all ingredients have been used. Top each dish with slices of Mozzarella cheese.
- Bake in 350°F. oven 30 minutes, or until bubbly-hot.

STEAK, KIDNEY AND MUSHROOM PIE   Serves 4

1½ pounds round steak, cut in inch
    or 1½ inch cubes
  1 beef kidney, cut in pieces
  3 tablespoons butter or margarine

½ pound fresh mushrooms, sliced
10 ounce can beef gravy
  2 tablespoons red wine
    pie dough recipe for 1 crust pie

- Sauté steak and kidney briefly in butter, then add mushrooms. Remove from heat, mix with gravy and red wine. Place in a pottery or enamel baking dish, round and shallow. Top with pastry.
- Bake in a 350°F. oven 25-30 minutes.

STIR FRY BEEF WITH GREEN PEPPER AND TOMATOES   Serves 4

1½ pounds beef sirloin or flank steak
  2 green peppers, cut into strips
  1 onion, sliced
  1 clove garlic, minced

1 tablespoon fat
1 tablespoon cornstarch
2 cups canned tomatoes
  salt and pepper

- Cut steak lengthwise with the grain, then slice against the grain, then in strips, about ¼ of an inch.
- Brown garlic in fat in a frying pan.
- Add onions and green peppers, stir until almost tender.
- Add sliced beef, stir until half done.
- Season to taste, add tomatoes.
- Cook until tender; mix a little cornstarch with cold water and add for thickening.

TERIYAKI   Serves 4

2 pounds sirloin tip, no fat, cut into
  strips ⅓ inch thick and
  2-3 inches long
1 cup soy sauce
⅓ cup water

2 tablespoons sugar
2 cloves garlic, minced
1 piece fresh ginger root, minced fine
2-3 tablespoons brandy

- Make a marinade of all the ingredients, soak slices of meat about 2 hours.
- Thread on bamboo or metal skewers (Bamboo skewers should be soaked in water first). Broil briefly.

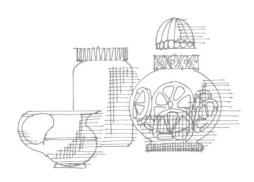

⟫VEAL SECTION⟪

BAKED VEAL WITH PEAS

Serves 5

1½ pounds thick veal steak or chops
2 tablespoons olive oil
2½ cups frozen peas

pepper
salt

- Put veal in a casserole with olive oil on the bottom.
- Add the frozen peas right from the package, and sprinkle with freshly ground black pepper. Cover tightly and bake in a 325°F. oven 1 hour.
- Just before serving, sprinkle with salt.

VEAL CHOPS IN MUSHROOM SAUCE

Serves 4

2 tablespoons cooking oil
4 thick veal rib chops
2 tablespoons flour
1 can beef gravy
⅓ cup sherry wine
1 tablespoon tomato paste

4 ounce can sliced mushrooms
or
¼ pound fresh mushrooms,
sliced and sautéed
⅛ teaspoon each thyme and marjoram
minced garlic, salt, pepper to taste

- Heat oil in a large frying pan, brown chops briefly on both sides.
- Remove chops from pan.
- Add flour stirring until well blended.
- Add beef gravy and wine; cook, stirring constantly, until mixture boils and thickens.
- Stir in tomato paste, mushrooms and seasonings.
- Add chops, cover, and bake in 350°F. oven for 1 hour, turn and baste chops several times.

VEAL GOULASH PAPRIKA

Serves 8

2 tablespoons butter or margarine
3 cups thinly sliced onions
3 pounds shoulder of veal,
cut in 1½ inch cubes
1 tablespoon paprika
1 teaspoon salt

1 cup hot beef broth
1 cup julienne cut green peppers
1 cup peeled, diced tomatoes
½ teaspoon caraway seeds
½ cup sour cream
cooked egg noodles

- Brown onions and meat in kettle over medium heat, stirring to brown all sides.
- Add paprika, salt and broth; cover and cook over low heat 30 minutes.
- Add green peppers, tomatoes and caraway seeds; recover and cook 30 minutes longer or until tender.
- Blend in sour cream; serve with noodles.

⇶ PORK SECTION ⇶

APPLE-STUFFED SPARERIBS — Serves 6 - 8

- Prepare Savory Apple Stuffing, spread on 1 strip (2 matching sides) of spareribs, cover with matching strip, tie firmly with string.
- Put in roasting pan with ½ cup hot water, season; cover and roast in 350°F. oven for 3 hours or until done, remove cover during last hour of roasting.

SAVORY APPLE STUFFING

½ cup chopped celery and leaves
1 onion, chopped
2 tablespoons chopped parsley
¼ cup butter or margarine
4 cups diced, peeled tart apples

¼ cup brown sugar, firmly packed
¾ teaspoon salt
¼ teaspoon each ground sage, marjoram, thyme, pepper
2 cups toasted bread crumbs

- Cook celery, onion and parsley in butter for 5 minutes.
- Add apples, sugar and seasonings; cook, stirring, for about 5 minutes; stir in bread crumbs.

AU GRATIN HAM AND SPINACH — Serves 4

2 10 ounce packages frozen spinach
8 slices cooked ham (not too thin)
2 tablespoons butter or margarine
2 tablespoons flour
⅓ cup chicken broth

½ cup light cream
⅓ cup grated Swiss cheese
⅓ cup freshly grated Parmesan cheese
2 tablespoons brandy
salt and pepper

- Let spinach thaw slightly, arrange a layer on the bottom of a medium-sized casserole, then 4 slices of ham, overlapping if necessary.
- Make a sauce by melting the butter, stirring in the flour, and cooking for a minute or two. Add chicken broth, a little at a time, stir until smooth, and then add the cream.
- Stir in the cheese, brandy, salt, and pepper, put half of the mixture on top of the ham.
- Add another layer of spinach and ham and top with the rest of the sauce.
- Bake in a 350°F. oven 20 minutes or until lightly browned.

BARBECUED PORK RIBS — Serves 8

6 pounds fresh pork ribs
4 onions, chopped
2 cups water
2 beef bouillon cubes
½ cup dark brown sugar
1 cup catsup
½ cup cider vinegar

2 cups tomato purée
1 tablespoon each garlic powder, celery salt, chili powder
½ teaspoon each ground allspice, cloves, ginger, mustard
½ cup drained sweet pickle relish

- Brown ribs in heavy kettle; add remaining ingredients.
- Cover, simmer for 2 hours or until tender.

CHEESE, HAM AND BROCCOLI CASSEROLE   Serves 8

1 cup uncooked regular rice
2 10 ounce packages frozen
  broccoli spears
6 tablespoons butter or margarine
2 cups fresh bread crumbs
2 large onions, chopped fine

3 tablespoons flour
⅓ teaspoon salt
¼ teaspoon pepper
3 cups milk
4 cups cooked ham, cubed
1 8 ounce package sliced process cheese

- Cook rice according to package directions; spoon into a greased 13 x 9 x 2 inch casserole.
- Cook broccoli, drain well. Place in a single layer over the rice.
- Melt butter in a large frying pan; measure out 2 tablespoons and sprinkle over bread crumbs; set aside.
- Stir onions into remaining butter in frying pan; sauté until soft.
- Stir in flour, salt and pepper; cook, stirring constantly, until bubbly.
- Stir in milk; continue cooking and stirring until sauce thickens and boils 1 minute.
- Stir in ham; heat again, just until bubbly; pour over layers in baking dish.
- Place cheese slices over sauce; sprinkle buttered bread crumbs over all. Cover; chill.
- Before serving, uncover dish; place in 350°F. oven.
- Bake 45 minutes, or until bubbly and crumb topping is golden.

HALF-HOUR PIZZA   2 14-inch pies

  vegetable oil
4 packages refrigerated crescent
  dinner rolls
  15 ounce can spaghetti sauce
1 can (about 3 or 4 ounces) sliced
  mushrooms, drained

½ cup sliced pitted ripe olives
1½ teaspoon leaf oregano, crumbled
1 8 ounce package Mozzarella
  cheese, shredded
1 pound brown'n'serve sausages,
  sliced diagonally

- Lightly oil two 14 inch round pizza pans. Open crescent rolls following label directions. Unroll and separate dough triangles. Fit triangles from 2 packages into each pizza pan.
- Spread half of spaghetti sauce on each pizza. Divide mushrooms and olives evenly over sauce; sprinkle with oregano. Sprinkle cheese over both pizzas.
- Arrange sausage slices in a pattern on the cheese.
- Bake in 400°F. oven 20 minutes, or until crusts are golden brown.
- Garnish with a sprig of fresh basil or parsley.

TO REHEAT FROZEN PIZZA: Bake in 400°F. oven for 30 minutes, or until filling is bubbly.

EASY SHEPHERD PIE

Serves 4

½ pound heat-and-serve sausage
   patties
2 tablespoons flour
2 cups water

1 envelope vegetable-beef soup mix
4 cups hot mashed potatoes
½ cup crumbled crackers
   chopped parsley

- Cut each sausage patty into about 10 small pieces; brown, stirring frequently, in a medium size frying pan

- Blend in flour; cook, stirring constantly, until bubbly.

- Stir in water and soup mix; continue cooking and stirring until gravy thickens and boils 5 minutes.

- Line bottom and sides of a buttered deep 1½ quart casserole with 3 cups of mashed potatoes.

- Spoon in sausage and gravy; spoon remaining potatoes in mounds over top; sprinkle with crumbled crackers.

- Bake in 350°F. oven, 45 minutes, or until bubbly-hot. Sprinkle with chopped parsley.

HAM AND CABBAGE WITH TOMATOES

Serves 4

½ medium cabbage, shredded
1 centre cut, uncooked ham slice,
   1 inch thick, cut in 4 serving pieces
2 cups canned tomatoes

½ teaspoon pepper
½ teaspoon monosodium glutamate
1 teaspoon steak sauce
1 teaspoon sugar

- Put cabbage in shallow 1½ quart baking dish.
- Arrange ham pieces on top.
- Mix remaining ingredients, spread on ham.
- Bake, uncovered in 350°F. oven for about 1 hour.
  Note: A fully cooked ham slice can be used in this recipe. Reduce cooking time to 45 minutes.

OLD WEST PORK CHOP CASSEROLE

Serves 6

6 pork chops, ¾ inch thick
2 tablespoons vegetable oil
1 large onion, cut into 6 slices
1 tablespoon chili powder
1 green pepper, chopped

1 cup uncooked regular rice
1 cup tomato sauce
1¼ cups water
1 teaspoon salt

- Brown chops well on both sides in oil; remove.

- Brown onion slices on both sides in same pan; remove.

- Stir in chili powder, cook 2 minutes; add green pepper, rice, tomato sauce, water and salt; heat to boiling.

- Pour into a shallow 2 quart casserole; arrange browned chops over rice and place an onion slice on each chop; cover dish.

- Bake in 375°F. oven 1 hour, or until liquid is absorbed.

ORIENTAL STYLE RIBS   Serves 6

4 to 5 pounds spareribs	1 tablespoon minced onion
2 tablespoons honey	1 small clove garlic, crushed
¼ cup Madeira wine	1 teaspoon salt
½ . cup soy sauce	½ teaspoon ground ginger
½ cup water	¼ teaspoon ground black pepper

- Cut meat between the ribs, but do not cut all the way through.
- Place meat in a long dish; combine remaining ingredients, pour over meat and marinate 4 to 5 hours or overnight, turning occasionally to marinate uniformly.
- Remove meat from marinade, reserving liquid; place meat on a rack in a large baking pan.
- Bake in a 350°F. oven 1½ hours or until meat is tender, basting frequently with the marinade.
- If desired, cook on a spit or on a rack over slow-burning charcoal about 1¼ hours, basting frequently.

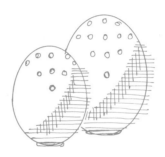

PORK CURRY   Serves 6

3 tablespoons lard or drippings	1 10 ounce can bouillon
1-1½ pounds boneless pork (from pork shoulder or pork butt, cut in cubes	½ cup water
	2 tablespoons curry powder
1 medium onion, chopped	1 teaspoon salt
¼ cup thinly sliced celery	½ cup raisins
1 clove garlic, crushed	2 apples, peeled, sliced
¼ cup flour	½ cup milk

- Heat lard or drippings in frypan.
- Brown pork cubes; remove and set aside.
- Cook onion, celery and garlic 4 minutes.
- Sprinkle in flour; stir and cook mixture about 2 minutes longer.
- Blend in bouillon, water, curry powder and salt. Add raisins, apple slices and pork cubes. Cover pan and simmer gently for 35-minutes (may be chilled or frozen until ready to use; then reheat).
- Just before serving, stir in milk and heat 2 minutes.
- Serve over hot, fluffy rice accompanied by condiments like chutney, salted peanuts, banana and orange slices.

PORK SHOULDER WITH PARSLEY SAUCE   Serves 10-12

5 pound smoked pork picnic shoulder
water
1 tablespoon mixed pickling spices

1 cup firmly packed brown sugar
1 cup apple juice
¼ teaspoon ground cloves
½ cup chopped parsley

- Place picnic shoulder in a kettle; add cold water to cover; add pickling spices.
- Heat slowly to boiling; reduce heat; cover; simmer 2½ hours, or until meat is tender. Remove from heat; allow meat to cool in liquid at least 30 minutes.
- Place picnic shoulder in a shallow roasting pan. Cut skin from top of meat; score fat.
- To make Parsley Sauce: Combine brown sugar, apple juice and cloves in a saucepan; heat to boiling; reduce heat; simmer 5 minutes.
- Remove sauce from heat; stir in chopped parsley, brush part of sauce over meat.
- Roast in 375°F. oven, basting several times with part of sauce, 30 minutes, or until well-glazed.

SAUSAGE AND POTATO PIE   Serves 4

4 cups mashed potatoes
2 tablespoons butter or margarine
2 eggs
3 tablespoons finely chopped parsley

1 large green pepper, seeds removed and coarsely chopped
1 pound lean pork sausage

- Lightly sauté sausage, add parsley and green pepper.
- Mix mashed potatoes with the unbeaten eggs and the butter.
- Put half the mixture in the bottom of a shallow casserole.
- Spread with the sausage mixture and top with the rest of the potatoes.
- Bake in 350°F. oven 35-40 minutes.

SPAGHETTI WITH MEATY SAUCE   Serves 8

2 tablespoons oil
1 clove garlic, crushed
1 teaspoon parsley
10 ounce can tomatoes

2 cups tomato paste
½ pound beef in one piece
1 pound fresh spareribs
½ pound Italian sausage

- Heat oil, add garlic and parsley. Sauté for a few minutes.
- Add tomatoes, tomato paste, and 1 cup water.
- Simmer 2 hours, stirring often.
- Brown beef, spareribs and sausage. Add to the tomato sauce and simmer for another hour or until meat is cooked.
- Serve over hot cooked spaghetti.

⇒ LAMB SECTION ⇐

CURRIED LAMB WITH GOLDEN PILAF   Serves 8

4 pounds stewing lamb, cut in
  pieces, reserve bones
2 cups water
2 tablespoons vegetable oil
3 cups cooking apples, pared,
  quartered, cored and chopped

1¼ cup celery, chopped
5 teaspoons curry powder
1 teaspoon salt
  Golden Pilaf (recipe follows)

- Place bones in water; heat to boiling; reduce heat; cover, simmer 30 minutes.
- Strain broth into a 2 cup measure (you should have 1½ cups); reserve.
- Brown lamb pieces slowly in oil in a frying pan; remove meat, reserve.
- Stir apple and celery into drippings in pan; sauté until soft; blend in curry powder, cook 1 minute.
- Stir in reserved lamb broth and salt. Heat to boiling; reduce heat; cover. Simmer 10 minutes.
- Mash this mixture with the back of a wooden spoon to make a smoother sauce.
- Return reserved meat to frying pan, cover; simmer 1 hour, or until meat is tender. Serve with Golden Pilaf.

GOLDEN PILAF

2 cups uncooked regular rice
¼ cup vegetable oil
1 cup onion, chopped

5 cups chicken broth or
  equivalent
½ cup golden raisins

- Sauté rice in oil until golden brown, stirring often; remove.
- Sauté onion until soft in remaining oil, return rice to pan with onion, chicken broth, salt, hot water and raisins.
- Heat to boiling; reduce heat to low; cover. Simmer 35 minutes, or until liquid is absorbed and rice is tender.

LAMB, ORANGE AND BARLEY

Serves 4

2 onions, chopped
2 tablespoons butter or margarine
1 pound lamb shoulder, cut in
   2 inch squares,
      or
2 cups diced cooked lamb

1 cup pearl barley
3 oranges, sliced thin, seeds removed
   but not peeled,
      or
1 tablespoon lemon juice
3 cups beef bouillon

- Sauté onions and lamb in butter. Put in a medium-sized casserole with barley, oranges and half the liquid.
- Cover and bake in 300°F. oven.
- Bake 45 minutes, add the rest of the bouillon, cover again, and bake 45 minutes longer or until done. Let stand 5-10 minutes before serving.

LAMB RIBLET CASSEROLE

Serves 6

4 pounds lamb riblets or breast of
   lamb, cut into serving size pieces
½ pound medium-size onions, peeled
   and quartered
2 teaspoons salt
1 teaspoon Worcestershire sauce
½ teaspoon leaf rosemary, crumbled
¼ teaspoon pepper
5 medium-size potatoes, pared and
   cut into 1 inch pieces

1 large pepper squash, peeled and
   cut into 1 inch pieces
3 green onions, washed and sliced
1 tablespoon butter or margarine
¼ cup flour
⅓ cup water
   parsley (optional)

- Brown lamb, a few pieces at a time in a kettle or Dutch oven, moving pieces as they brown. Sauté onions in drippings, 10 minutes, or until nicely browned. Remove; reserve.
- Return meat to kettle; add water, salt, Worcestershire, rosemary and pepper; heat to boiling; lower heat; cover; simmer 30 minutes.
- Add potatoes and onions, pushing them down under liquid. Simmer 40 minutes longer, or until meat and potatoes are tender.
- Meanwhile sauté onions in butter only until tender.
- Lift out meat and vegetables, arrange on a shallow heated serving dish along with onion; cover and keep warm.
- Let fat rise to top of meat-vegetable broth; skim off all possible fat; heat to boiling.
- Blend flour and water in a small cup; stir into boiling broth.
- Cook and stir until gravy thickens and bubbles 1 minute. Pour over lamb. Sprinkle with chopped parsley.

MOUSSAKA   Serves 6

2 1¼ pound eggplants, halved
    lengthwise
2 cups chopped onion
1 clove garlic, minced
3 tablespoons olive or vegetable oil
½ pound fresh mushrooms, chopped

2 cups cooked lamb
2 teaspoons salt
½ teaspoon leaf oregano, crumbled
3 eggs
2 cups soft white bread crumbs

- Place eggplant, cut side down, in a 15 x 10 x 1 inch baking pan; pour boiling water in pan to a depth of one-half inch.
- Bake in 375°F. oven 30 minutes, or until eggplant is soft when pressed with fingertip. Remove eggplant from baking pan; drain on paper toweling.
- Scoop out inside of eggplant, being careful not to break the skin. Chop eggplant into small pieces.
- Sauté onion and garlic in oil, in frying pan, until soft; add mushrooms; sauté 3 minutes. Add eggplant and sauté until liquid in pan has evaporated. Stir in lamb, salt, pepper and oregano; cook 3 minutes; remove from heat.
- Beat eggs in a large bowl; stir in bread crumbs, then eggplant mixture, until well blended.
- Line an 8 cup charlotte mold or straight sided mold with eggplant shells, skin side out; spoon eggplant-lamb mixture into shells; fold shells over mixture. Cover mold with a double thickness of foil.
- Place mold on a rack or trivet in a kettle or steamer; pour in boiling water to half the depth of the mold.
- Bake in 375°F. oven 1 hour and 30 minutes; remove mold from water and remove foil cover; allow to stand on wire rack 10 minutes.
- Unmold onto heated serving platter, remove any excess moisture from platter.
- Garnish with chopped parsley and tomato. Serve immediately.

TWIN-MEAT CASSEROLE
Serves 16

3 pounds lean boneless lamb shoulder, cut in 1 inch cubes
3 pounds veal shoulder, cut into 1 inch cubes
2 large onions, peeled, sliced thin
1 large head iceberg lettuce, shredded
2 teaspoons salt
½ teaspoon pepper

1½ teaspoons leaf rosemary, crumbled
6 cups chicken broth or equivalent
16 medium-size potatoes, pared
2 pounds frozen peas
4 medium-size pepper squash sliced
2 cups cherry tomatoes
1 tablespoon butter or margarine
¼ cup cornstarch

- Combine first 8 ingredients; heat to boiling; cover, simmer 1 hour.

- Add potatoes, simmer 1 hour longer.

- About 15 minutes before meats are cooked, cook peas and squash in boiling salted water in seperate saucepans, until crisply tender; drain.

- Sauté tomatoes in butter until hot; shaking pan often.

- Blend cornstarch and about ½ cup water to a paste in a cup; stir into stew mixture. Cook, stirring constantly, until mixture thickens and boils 3 minutes.

- Spoon stew mixture into two heated large serving dishes; add squash slices, then peas, in squash rings. Pile tomatoes in centre.

- Garnish each tomato with a sprig of fresh rosemary.

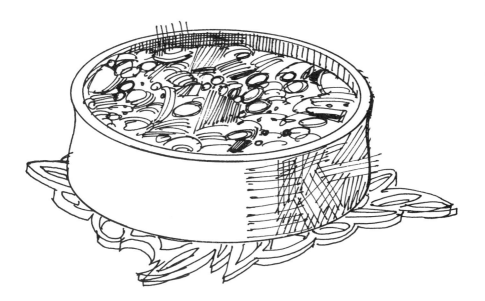

⇒ POULTRY SECTION ⇐

BREAST OF TURKEY ITALIENNE   Serves 6

3 small half breasts of turkey,
  skinned, boned and flattened slightly
  flour
2 eggs, beaten
2 cups fresh bread crumbs
6 tablespoons butter

6 thin slices Gruyére cheese,
  cut size of turkey breasts
6 thin slices smoked ham
½ cup tomato sauce
  salt and pepper

- Season the breasts lightly with salt and pepper; dust with flour, dip in beaten egg, and then cover generously with bread crumbs.
- Heat butter in a large frying pan over fairly high heat; brown the breasts for 4 minutes on one side; turn, brown for 3 minutes. (Test for doneness by pressing with the finger. If flesh is still soft, cook a little longer; if it feels slightly springy to the touch, it is fully cooked.)
- Transfer immediately to the rack of a broiler, cover each with a slice of cheese and ham; broil under a very hot flame for 1 minute to melt the cheese.
- Arrange on a hot serving platter; top each with a spoonful of tomato sauce.

Variations:

BREAST OF TURKEY WITH LEMON
- Omit cheese, ham and tomato sauce.
- Cover cooked turkey breasts with butter from pan and lemon juice.
- Garnish with parsley and lemon quarters.

BREAST OF TURKEY NERO
- Omit cheese, ham and tomato sauce.
- Place hot turkey on serving platter; add ½ cup brandy to pan; heat, ignite and pour flaming over breasts.

BREAST OF TURKEY PARMESAN
- Omit cheese, ham and tomato sauce.
- Place cooked turkey on hot platter.
- Add ½ cup Marsala wine to stock, cook to one-half quantity.
- Sprinkle ¾ cup grated Parmesan cheese over turkey breasts, place under broiler to melt cheese and sprinkle sliced truffle on top.
- Pour hot sauce over all.

Variations (continued)

BREAST OF TURKEY MEUNIERE
- Omit cheese, ham and tomato sauce.
- Place cooked turkey breasts on heated platter.
- Add 1 tablespoon butter and juice of 2 lemons to pan juice; heat, pour over turkey.

CALICO CHICKEN   Serves 4

2½ pound broiler-fryer chicken
3 tablespoons vegetable oil
1 large onion, chopped
1 clove of garlic, minced
1 cup uncooked rice
2¼ cups water

2 cups frozen mixed vegetables
2 envelopes instant chicken broth
   or bouillon cubes
1 teaspoon salt
1½ teaspoons leaf tarragon, crumbled

- Cut chicken into serving-size pieces. Brown well on all sides in oil in a large frying pan; remove chicken from pan and reserve.
- Sauté onion and garlic until soft in same pan. Stir in rice, brown 3 minutes.
- Stir in water, frozen vegetables, instant chicken broth, salt and tarragon. Add chicken. Heat to boiling. Lower heat; cover.
- Simmer 30 minutes, or until chicken is tender and liquid is absorbed.

CHICKEN MARENGO   Serves 6

3½ pounds chicken legs and breasts
1 teaspoon salt
½ teaspoon black pepper
   flour
¼ cup olive oil or salad oil
3 tablespoons butter or margarine
1 cup chicken stock or water
12 small white onions, peeled

½ cup sliced green pepper
4 tomatoes, peeled, seeded and
   quartered
½ cup pitted black olives
⅛ teaspoon ground allspice
¼ pound sliced mushrooms
½ cup dry white wine

- Rub chicken with salt and pepper; dredge in flour.
- Brown in ¼ cup oil and 2 tablespoons butter; add next 6 ingredients; cover and simmer 45 minutes or until chicken is tender.
- Sauté mushrooms in remaining butter; add to chicken along with wine 5 minutes before cooking time is up.
- Serve with rice.

CHICKEN PAPRIKA

Serves 8

2 3 pound broiler-fryers
2 tablespoons butter or margarine
1 large onion, chopped
3 tablespoons paprika
1 tablespoon flour
2 teaspoons salt

¼ teaspoon pepper
1 cup tomatoes
1 pound noodles, cooked
1 cup dairy sour cream
1½ tablespoons chopped parsley

- Cut chickens into serving-size pieces.
- Sauté onion in butter until soft; stir in paprika and flour; cook, stirring constantly, 1 minute.
- Stir in salt, pepper and tomatoes.
- Add chicken and giblets (except livers), turning to coat pieces well; cover; simmer 30 minutes. Turn; add livers; simmer 15 minutes longer, or until chicken is tender.
- Spoon hot noodles onto heated platter. Remove chicken from pan with a slotted spoon. Arrange on noodles; keep warm.
- Spoon sour cream into a medium size bowl. Heat sauce in pan to boiling; stir slowly into sour cream, blend well. Spoon over chicken.
- Garnish with parsley.

CHICKEN POT PIE

Serves 4

1 cup water
⅓ cup dry milk solids
2 tablespoons flour
¾ teaspoon salt
¼ teaspoon tarragon
¼ teaspoon parsley
⅛ teaspoon pepper
2 cups cooked cubed chicken
(approx. ¾ pound)

½ cup cooked onion
½ cup cooked carrot slices
½ cup cooked lima beans
½ cup cooked peas
⅓ cup flour
dash salt
1½ tablespoons butter or margarine
1½ tablespoons water

- Combine first 7 ingredients, beat until smooth; cook over medium heat stirring constantly until mixture comes to a boil.
- Fold in next 5 ingredients; pour into 1½ quart casserole.
- Combine flour and salt; cut in butter or margarine with a pastry blender or two knives and water and blend in with folk. Roll out to cover casserole.
- Place over casserole, crimp edges firmly to edge of casserole; cut pastry top with fork.
- Bake in 400°F. oven for 20 minutes.

CHICKEN RISOTTO

Serves 4

2 tablespoons thinly sliced
green onion
1 tablespoon butter or margarine
1½ cups chopped celery
1¼ cups packaged precooked rice
1 can condensed cream of chicken
soup
1½ cups milk

1½ tablespoons soy sauce
1½ cups diced cooked chicken
1 3-4 ounce can chopped mushrooms,
drained
1 2 ounce can or jar pimientos,
drained and sliced
3 ounces chow-mein
noodles

- Sauté onion in butter until soft; stir in celery and rice; cook 1 minute longer.
- Stir in soup, milk, soy sauce, chicken, mushrooms and pimientos; heat to boiling. Spoon into a 1½ quart casserole; cover.
- Bake in 375°F. oven 20 minutes; uncover. Sprinkle noodles over top.
- Bake 10 minutes longer, or until noodles are hot.

CHICKEN, TOMATO AND OLIVES

Serves 4

2½-3 pound chicken, split,
flattened and quartered
¼ cup olive oil
¼ cup melted butter or margarine

4 large ripe tomatoes, peeled, quartered
10 large ripe olives and 10 large
green olives, pitted
salt and pepper

- Season chicken, place in a shallow baking dish, drizzle with oil.
- Bake uncovered in a 400°F. oven about 25 minutes, basting from time to time with the olive oil and juices in the pan.
- Remove and transfer to a warm platter.
- Pour melted butter over.
- Meanwhile, cook tomatoes in their juices for 4 or 5 minutes, add the olives and pour over the chicken pieces.

DELUXE CHICKEN TETRAZZINI   Serves 8

3½ - 4 pound chicken
  3 cups water
1½ teaspoons salt
  ½ teaspoon celery salt
  ½ teaspoon onion powder
  8 ounce package egg noodles
  6 tablespoons butter or margarine
  ½ pound fresh mushrooms, sliced
    (optional)

1 tablespoon lemon juice
3 tablespoons flour
½ teaspoon salt
¼ teaspoon paprika
¼ teaspoon pepper
⅛ teaspoon nutmeg
1 cup whipping cream
⅔ cup grated Parmesan cheese
  paprika

- Cook first 5 ingredients until chicken is tender, approximately one hour.
- Remove chicken, break into large pieces.
- Reserve broth (if necessary, add water to make 2 cups).
- Cook noodles according to package directions. Drain and put in a 9 x 13 x 2 inch baking dish.
- Arrange chicken pieces on top.
- Sauté mushrooms in 3 tablespoons butter; add lemon juice, put aside.
- In a large saucepan, melt 3 tablespoons butter, add flour, salt, paprika, pepper and nutmeg. Mix well. Gradually stir in broth, and cook until thickened; add cream and sautéed mushrooms.
- Pour over chicken.
- Top with grated cheese and paprika.
- Bake in 400°F. oven for 25 minutes.

DICED CHICKEN WITH ALMONDS   Serves 4

3 tablespoons cooking oil
1 teaspoon salt
2 cups diced raw chicken
2 tablespoons soy sauce
1 cup cooked peas
1 cup diced celery

⅓ cup canned mushrooms
1 cup boiling water
1 tablespoon cornstarch
¼ cup cold water
⅓ cup toasted almonds

- Heat oil and salt in a wok or deep frying pan; when very hot add chicken and sauté or stir fry for 3 minutes.
- Season with soy sauce and stir well.
- Add peas, celery, mushrooms, and boiling water very slowly; stir well; cover pan and cook 4 minutes.
- Add cornstarch mixed with cold water, lower heat.
- When the gravy thickens and becomes clear, remove from heat and transfer to a shallow plate.
- Sprinkle with toasted almonds. Serve very hot.

EASY STUFFED CHICKEN BREASTS

Serves 8

4 whole chicken breasts (about. 12 oz. each) halved
6 ounces process Gruyère cheese, shredded
¼ pound salami, diced
½ cup chopped green onions
1 egg
1 package seasoned mix for chicken
¼ cup butter or margarine
¼ cup flour
2 cups milk

- Remove skin from breast, cut meat in one piece from bones.
- Place each chicken breast between two sheets or wax paper and pound with a wooden mallet.
- Combine 1 cup of the cheese, salami and green onions in small bowl.
- Place about ¼ cup of the cheese filling in the centre of each chicken breast.
- Roll up tightly and fasten with a pick.
- Beat egg in a shallow dish; place seasoned coating mix on wax paper. Dip stuffed breast in egg; roll in seasoned coating mix. Place in single layer in greased baking dish.
- Bake in 400°F. oven 40 minutes, or until golden brown.
- While chicken is baking, make cheese sauce. Melt butter in a medium size saucepan; stir in flour; cook, stirring constantly just until bubbly.
- Stir in milk, continue cooking and stirring until sauce thickens and bubbles 1 minute; stir in remaining cheese until melted. Serve with chicken.

HOMEMADE CHICKEN PIE

Serves 6

2½-3 pound chicken
10 small onions
3 whole allspice
1 cup white wine
¼ teaspoon nutmeg
12 peppercorns
2 tablespoons butter or margarine
1½ tablespoons cornstarch
3 tablespoons lemon juice
1 egg yolk, slightly beaten
2 hard-cooked eggs, sliced
⅓ pound diced cooked or uncooked ham
Pastry for top of pie

- Pull meat from the carcass of chicken before cooking, cut into bite-size pieces.
- Put in a shallow pan, heat the pieces of chicken with the onions, allspice, white wine, 2 cups of water, nutmeg and peppercorns, simmer, covered, for about 20 minutes until the chicken and the onions are partially done and the liquid slightly reduced.
- Remove peppercorns and allspice.
- Add the sliced hard-cooked eggs and diced ham.
- Cook remaining liquid with butter and cornstarch mixed with the lemon juice until slightly thickened. Remove from the fire and add a little of the hot liquid to the slightly beaten egg yolk. Blend well with the rest of the thickened liquid and pour over the ingredients in the pie dish. Top with the pastry and bake in a 350°F. oven for 45 minutes.

MANDARIN BAKED CHICKEN   Serves 4

¼ cup water
¼ cup soy sauce
¼ cup dry sherry
¼ cup corn syrup

1 teaspoon seasoned salt
3 pound broiler-fryer chicken,
  quartered

- Combine first 5 ingredients in bowl.
- Arrange chicken skin side up, on rack in broiler pan or shallow baking pan with a rack. Brush generously with part of the soy-sherry sauce.
- Bake in 350°F. oven for 1½ hours, basting with remaining sauce every 20 minutes, until chicken is tender and deep golden brown. Place chicken on a heated serving platter.

ORIENTAL CHICKEN PILAF   Serves 6

3 pounds chicken pieces
  salt
  black pepper
6 tablespoons butter or margarine
½ cup chopped onion
1 cup long-grain rice

2½ cups hot chicken stock or water
¼ teaspoon saffron
1 green pepper, cut into strips
2 tomatoes, quartered, peeled
  and seeded
¼ teaspoon black pepper

- Rub chicken pieces with salt and pepper.
- Brown chicken and onions over moderate heat in 4 tablespoons of butter.
- Brown rice in remaining 2 tablespoons butter until it begins to stick to bottom of pan; add to chicken with 1 teaspoon salt and remaining ingredients.
- Turn into a 2 quart casserole; cover and bake in 350°F. oven 20 to 25 minutes or until chicken and rice are tender and the rice has absorbed most of the liquid.
- Serve with the chicken arranged over the rice.

PARTY CHILI CHICKEN   Serves 8-12

8 ounces uncooked medium
  noodles
¼ cup chopped onion
1 tablespoon butter or margarine
10 ounce can condensed
  cream of mushroom soup
2 tablespoons chopped pimiento

1 tablespoon finely chopped
  green pepper
1½ cups cooked chicken or
  turkey, cut-up
  salt
  pepper
3 ounces grated Cheddar cheese

- Cook noodles as directed on package, drain.
- In large frying pan cook onion in butter until tender and stir in soup, pimiento and chopped pepper.
- In a greased 2 quart casserole layer half of the noodles and half the chicken, season with salt and pepper.
- Top with half the soup mixture and half the cheese.
- Repeat layers.
- Bake uncovered in 350°F. oven for 45 minutes.

STUFFED CHICKEN BREASTS   Serves 4

4 large breasts of chicken   3 tablespoons butter or margarine
  (2 whole breasts, split)   salt and pepper
2 chicken legs   flour and bread crumbs
1 egg

- Skin breasts, carefully remove the bones, pound very thin, between two pieces of waxed paper.
- Remove the skin from the two legs, cut the meat from the bone, dice.
- Put diced leg meat in a blender with half the butter, salt, and pepper.
- Divide into four parts and mold each part with your fingers into a two-inch long slender sausage.
- Wrap each breast around one of these, tucking in the ends, skewer closed with poultry nails or toothpicks.
- Roll each stuffed chicken breast in the flour and then in the egg beaten with 2 tablespoons of cold water, then again in the bread crumbs.
- Chill for several hours before sautéeing in a frying pan in the rest of the butter, place in a 350°F. oven for 15 minutes.

STUFFED CHICKEN BREASTS   Serves 4

4 slices of ham   4 whole breasts of chicken, boned
  or   4 slices Swiss or Cheddar cheese
8 slices back bacon

- Place a piece of ham or two pieces of back bacon on each chicken breast.
- Lay a slice of cheese on top of the ham.
- Roll the chicken, ham, and cheese together, tuck in the edges, and place in a shallow buttered casserole.
- Dot the top with butter and sprinkle with poultry seasoning.
- Bake in a 350°F. oven 1 hour, or until fork tender.

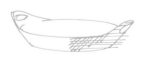

THE BRIDES FAVOURITE   Serves 4

3 pound broiler-fryer   3 or 4 ounce can chopped
1 can condensed cream of   mushrooms
  mushroom soup   ¼ cup water
1 large onion, chopped   2 tablespoons lemon juice

- Cut chicken into serving size pieces; arrange in a single layer in a 13 x 9 x 2 inch baking dish.
- Combine soup, onion, mushrooms and liquid, water and lemon juice in a medium size bowl. Spoon over chicken pieces.
- Bake in 375°F. oven 1 hour, or until chicken is tender and richly browned.

≫VARIETY MEAT SECTION≪

BACON AND LIVER CASSEROLE   Serves 8

6 slices bacon, diced
1 large onion, chopped
½ cup all purpose flour
¾ teaspoon salt
  dash of pepper
2 pounds sliced beef liver
  (cut into serving size pieces)

2½ cups milk
½ cup packaged bread crumbs
2 tablespoons butter or
  margarine, melted

- Combine bacon and onion in a large frying pan. Cook until bacon is crisp and onion is tender. Remove, reserving drippings.
- Combine flour, salt and pepper; coat liver. Reserve remaining flour mixture.
- Sauté liver in reserved bacon drippings; place in 2 quart casserole.
- Blend reserved flour mixture with drippings in pan; add milk. Cook over medium heat, stir constantly, until sauce thickens and bubbles.
- Pour sauce over liver; sprinkle with bacon and onion mixture.
- Combine bread crumbs with butter; sprinkle evenly over casserole.
- Bake in 350°F. oven for 25 minutes, or until sauce is bubbly.

CALF'S LIVER WITH PINEAPPLE   Serves 4

1 pound calf's liver
¼ cup soy sauce
12 ounce can pineapple juice
¼ cup cider vinegar
¼ teaspoon salt
¼ cup sugar

2 tablespoons cornstarch
8 ounce can pineapple chunks,
  drained
½ cup blanched almonds
¼ cup vegetable oil

- Cut' liver into narrow strips, dry.
- Combine next 6 ingredients; cook over low heat, stirring constantly until thickened and smooth.
- Add pineapple chunks and almonds; keep warm.
- Sauté liver in hot oil; heap on a hot serving dish and pour sauce over; serve with rice.

CALICO FRANKS   Serves 4

3 cups frozen vegetables
10 ounce can condensed cream of
    mushroom soup
1 cup milk

1 pound wieners, sliced
1 cup soft bread crumbs
1 cup shredded Cheddar cheese

- Combine frozen vegetables, soup and milk in a large saucepan; stir in wieners; spoon half into a 1½ quart casserole.
- Mix bread crumbs and cheese in a small bowl; sprinkle half over layer in baking dish. Top with remaining vegetable mixture, then remaining crumb mixture.
- Bake in 375°F. oven, 30 minutes, or until casserole is bubbly.

CHICKEN LIVER WITH PIMIENTO RICE   Serves 4

1½ pounds chicken livers
    flour
2 tablespoons butter or bacon
    drippings

10 ounce can beef gravy plus
¼ cup red wine

Pimiento Rice

10 ounce box rice seasoned
    with saffron
2½ cups chicken broth

2 cans whole pimientos, cut in strips
½ small can water chestnuts,
    drained and sliced thin

- Cut chicken livers in half, dust lightly with flour, sauté briefly in fat.
- Add beef gravy with wine, keep warm.
- Put the rice and chicken broth in a pan, bring to a broil, cover tightly, turn heat down very low.
- Cook 15-20 minutes.
- Remove from the heat, fluff with a fork.
- Stir in the pimiento strips and water chestnuts.
- Put chicken livers and sauce in centre of a hot platter or shallow casserole. Spoon the rice, pimiento and water chestnut mixture around the edges.

DINNER IN A DISH   Serves 4

1 cup sliced celery
3 hard-cooked eggs, halved
1½ cups cubed cooked meat
3 tablespoons butter or margarine
3 tablespoons flour
1 teaspoon salt

¼ teaspoon pepper
1½ cups milk
1 onion, thinly sliced
2 tablespoons chopped green pepper
    (optional)
Cheese Crescents – see recipe page 191.

- Arrange celery, eggs and meat in ungreased baking pan 8 x 8 x 2 inches.
- Melt butter over low heat, blend in flour, salt and pepper; cook stirring until mixture is smooth and bubbly; remove from heat.
- Stir in milk, heat to boiling stirring constantly for 1 minute and then stir in onion and green pepper.
- Pour over meat and top with Cheese Crescents. Bake in 425°F. oven for 25-30 minutes.

FRIED SWEETBREADS WITH MUSHROOMS AND BACON
Serves 8

4 pairs parboiled calf's sweetbreads,
  sliced, ½ inch slices
½ cup dry bread crumbs
1 teaspoon salt

¼ teaspoon black pepper
¾ pound mushrooms, halved
3 tablespoons butter or margarine
8 slices crisp bacon

- Dip sweetbreads into mixture of bread crumbs, salt and pepper.
- Cook mushrooms, covered, in 2 tablespoons butter for 5 minutes; remove, keep warm.
- Sauté sweetbreads in remaining butter.
- Arrange on a hot platter and surround with the bacon and mushrooms.

TONGUE AND RICE CASSEROLE
Serves 6

¼ cup uncooked rice
2½ cups frozen peas, cooked and
  drained
2 cups cubed, cooked, tongue
1 can condensed Cheddar cheese soup

1 cup milk
¼ teaspoon salt
⅛ teaspoon pepper
⅓ cup croûtons

- Cook rice, according to package directions.
- Combine rice, peas and tongue in a shallow 2 quart casserole.
- Blend cheese soup with milk in a medium size bowl; add salt and pepper. Pour over rice mixture. Toss lightly to mix. Arrange croûtons around edge of dish.
- Bake in 375° F. oven 30 minutes, or until sauce is bubbly and the top is lightly browned.

SUPPER CASSEROLE
Serves 4

2 cups soft bread cubes
2 ounces grated Cheddar cheese
2 tablespoons butter or margarine,
  melted
1 cup cooked peas or other vegetable
3 tablespoons chopped onion
2 tablespoons butter or margarine

2 tablespoons flour
¾ teaspoon salt
⅛ teaspoon pepper
1½ cups milk
1 cup cut up cooked meat
1 large tomato, sliced

- Mix bread cubes, cheese and 2 tablespoons butter. Spread ½ of the mixture in a greased 1 quart casserole and top with peas.
- Cook and stir onion in 2 tablespoons butter until onion is tender.
- Blend in flour and seasonings.
- Cook over low heat stirring until mixture is bubbly.
- Remove from heat, stir in milk and heat to boiling stirring constantly; boil and stir 1 minute.
- Stir in meat; pour over peas; arrange tomato slices on top and sprinkle with remaining bread mixture.
- Bake uncovered in 350°F. oven for 25 minutes.

GROUND & CUBED
MEAT SPECIALS
FOR
FAMILY AND FRIENDS

Ground meats of all kinds, plain or in combination with each other, mix perfectly with countless combinations of foods, herbs and spices.

Ground meats give the artistic and creative cooks an opportunity to shine with something new every time.

Tender, economical, flavourful—they can be baked, braised, broiled, barbecued, pan-fried or stewed.

Ground meats are the versatile friend of all homemakers and gourmets.

⇒BEEF SECTION⇐

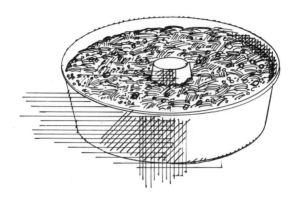

BAKED MEAT LOAF RING   Serves 8

1½ pounds lean ground beef
  4 slices bread, soaked in ½ cup milk,
    squeezed dry
  ½ cup freshly grated Parmesan cheese
  ⅓ cup finely chopped parsley
    4 ounce jar whole pimientos,
    cut in ½ inch squares

1 teaspoon grated orange peel
1 teaspoon oregano
2 teaspoons Worcestershire sauce
1 teaspoon salt, or according to taste
2 eggs

- Mix all the ingredients together, pat into a greased, 5-cup ring mold. Bake in a 350°F. oven about an hour.

BEEF CRUST PIE   Serves 6

Meat Mixture
  1 pound ground beef
  ½ cup rolled oats
  ⅓ cup finely chopped onion
  ¼ cup diced green pepper
  ⅓ cup shredded carrot
  2 tablespoons chopped fresh parsley
  ¾ teaspoon salt

  ⅛ teaspoon pepper
  ¼ teaspoon savory
  1 egg, beaten
  ½ cup tomato juice
  1 tablespoon tomato catsup
  1 teaspoon Worcestershire sauce

- Mix beef, rolled oats, vegetables and seasonings.
- Combine egg with remaining ingredients. Add to beef and mix well.
- Press mixture on bottom and sides of 9-inch pie plate, flute edges.

Filling
  2 cups cooked rice
  1 cup tomato sauce
  ⅛ teaspoon pepper

  ⅛ teaspoon basil
  1 cup grated Cheddar cheese

- Combine rice, tomato sauce, seasonings and ¼ cup of grated cheese.
- Spread filling in meat shell, cover and bake in 350°F. oven 25 minutes.
- Uncover, sprinkle with remaining ¾ cup cheese, bake uncovered until cheese melts (10 to 15 minutes).

BEEF RING   Serves 8

2 pounds ground beef
½ cup chopped onion
2 cups fresh bread crumbs
½ cup soft butter or margarine
2 teaspoons salt

½ teaspoon black pepper
½ teaspoon dry mustard
2 tablespoons minced parsley
½ cup chili sauce

- Mix together thoroughly all ingredients but chili sauce.
- Pack into greased 9-inch ring mold; spread chili sauce on top.
- Bake in a 400°F. oven 45 minutes or until meat is browned and shrunk away from sides of the pan.
- Turn out onto a hot serving dish; fill the centre with creamed vegetables or mushrooms.

BEEF BALLS IN PINEAPPLE SAUCE   Serves 6

1½ pounds ground beef
¼ cup finely chopped onion
1 egg
1 teaspoon salt
⅛ teaspoon black pepper
¼ cup flour
2 tablespoons shortening

1 cup beef broth
2 tablespoons lemon juice
1 lemon, thinly sliced
4 tablespoons brown sugar
1 teaspoon salt
¼ cup gingersnap crumbs
8 ounce can pineapple chunks

- Mix first 6 ingredients; form into 1 inch balls; lightly roll in flour.
- Brown meat balls on all sides.
- Drain the pineapple and reserve ½ cup of juice.
- Add next five ingredients; cover and cook over low heat 35 minutes.
- Stir in gingersnap crumbs; add pineapple and cook 10 minutes longer.

Variations:

BURGUNDY MEATBALLS IN RAISIN SAUCE

- Add ⅓ cup milk and ¼ cup dry bread crumbs to meatballs; brown; remove.
  Sauce — In drippings blend in 1½ tablespoons flour and ¼ teaspoon garlic powder. Add 1 cup beef broth, 2 tablespoons tomato paste and ½ cup seedless raisins.
  Add meatballs, cover and simmer 30 minutes.
  Remove meatballs, stir in ¼ cup dry red wine, heat and pour over meatballs.

PEANUTTY BURGER BALLS

- Add ¾ cup peanut butter to meat mixture; brown as above.
- Pour 2 cups tomato sauce over meatballs; cover and simmer 30 minutes.

CURRIED MEAT BALLS

- Add ½ cup juice from canned tomatoes and 1 cup soft bread crumbs to meatball mixture.
- Add 3 cups canned tomatoes, 1 teaspoon seasoned salt, ½ teaspoon sugar and 1 teaspoon curry powder.
- Bring to boil, cover and simmer 20 - 25 minutes.
- Serve over hot rice.

CHILI CON CARNE

Serves 4

¾ pound chopped beef
1 clove garlic, minced
3 small onions, sliced
2 cups canned tomatoes

1 teaspoon salt
2 teaspoons chili powder
4 cups red kidney beans

- Combine first 3 ingredients in a large frying pan and fry slowly for about 10 minutes.
- Add remaining ingredients and simmer for 10 minutes longer.
- Serve with crackers and shredded lettuce.

Note: To make chili spicier, add a pinch of crushed red pepper and more chili powder.

BEEF SCRAMBLE

Serves 4

1 cup elbow macaroni
1 large onion, chopped
1 tablespoon vegetable oil
1 pound ground beef

1 19 ounce can chunky vegetable soup
1 tablespoon chopped parsley
¾ teaspoon seasoned salt
¼ teaspoon pepper

- Cook macaroni in boiling, salted water, following label directions; drain, reserve.
- Sauté onion in vegetable oil until soft in a large frying pan; crumble ground beef into pan, continue cooking until pink is gone from meat.
- Stir in vegetable soup, parsley, salt, pepper and macaroni. Heat until bubbly.

CHILI CON CARNE

Serves 6

1 cup chopped onion
1 tablespoon fat
1½ pounds ground beef
1 tablespoon chili powder
¾ teaspoon salt

¼ teaspoon pepper
½ teaspoon oregano
2 10 ounce cans condensed
  tomato soup
2 14 ounce cans kidney beans

- Sauté onion in fat until transparent.
- Add beef and brown.
- Add remaining ingredients. Cover and simmer until thickened (about 20 minutes).

FLUFFY SWEDISH BEEF BALLS

Serves 6

6 eggs, separated
1 pound ground beef
1 teaspoon salt
¼ teaspoon black pepper
½ teaspoon baking powder

¼ cup grated onion
2 tablespoons minced parsley
¼ teaspoon thyme
½ cup shortening

- Beat egg yolks until thickened; add rest of ingredients.
- Fold in egg whites.
- Heat shortening; drop meat mixture into it by tablespoons.
- Fry until puffed and brown around the edges, then turn to brown other side.

EASTERN CURRY

Serves 8

3 pounds cubed beef and pork
4 onions, chopped
3 cloves garlic, minced
¼ cup cooking oil or fat from the meat
¼ cup coriander seeds
¼ cup ground cumin
3 bouillon cubes
⅔ can evaporated milk

1 tablespoon anchovy paste
½ teaspoon pepper
½ teaspoon chili powder
grated rind of ½ lemon
3 cups milk or dry skimmed milk, diluted
1 cup coconut, shredded
⅓ cup chopped mint leaves

- Sauté beef and pork in a frying pan, transfer to another container.
- Sauté onion and garlic in the same pan.
- Rub the coriander and cumin between your palms, letting the heat of your hands warm it.
- Add to onions and garlic, cook a bit in the fat.
- Add bouillon cubes, canned milk, anchovy paste, lemon rind and seasonings. Let simmer awhile, adding the milk as it starts to dry out.
- Add the beef and pork cubes, cook for 1-2 hours, or more. About ½ or ¾ hour before serving, add the coconut and mint leaves.

GROUND BEEF CURRY

Serves 6

2 tablespoons butter or margarine
1 cup chopped onion
1½ pounds ground beef
½ cup boiling water   OR
   beef broth

1 teaspoon salt
½ teaspoon black pepper
1 tablespoon curry powder
1 egg, beaten
1 cup plain yogurt

- Sauté the onion 10 minutes; stir in beef until browned.
- Add water, salt, pepper and curry powder; cover and cook over low heat 15 minutes.
- Blend egg and yogurt gradually to meat mixture, stirring constantly, cook over low heat 5 minutes, do not let boil.
- Serve with rice.

HAMBURG COTTAGE CHEESE PIE

Serves 5

¾ cup chopped onion
¼ cup finely chopped green pepper
2 tablespoons butter or margarine
1 pound ground beef
½ teaspoon salt
¼ teaspoon pepper

1 teaspoon Worcestershire sauce
2 tablespoons flour
1 baked 9 inch pie shell
1 cup cottage cheese
2 beaten eggs
dash paprika

- Sauté onion and green pepper in butter until onion is transparent.
- Add meat, brown.
- Stir in seasonings and flour.
- Spread meat mixture on pie shell.
- Blend cottage cheese with eggs and pour over meat.
- Sprinkle with paprika. Bake at 350°F. until brown (about 40 minutes).

MEAT BALLS AND SOUR CREAM   Serves 4

2 onions, chopped
3 tablespoons butter or margarine
1 pound ground beef
⅓ pound mushrooms, sliced
2 slices dry bread

salt and pepper
1 teaspoon sugar
1 egg
flour
1 cup sour cream

- Sauté onions in 1 tablespoon butter, until lightly browned.
- Remove mix with meat.
- In the same pan, sauté the mushrooms in a little butter (3-5 minutes) stir; remove from the heat.
- Soak the dry bread in water, squeeze out.
- Mix the onions, meat and soaked bread; add salt, pepper, sugar and egg, mix.
- Shape into about 12 meat balls, dust lightly in flour. Brown in butter on each side.
- Add the sour cream and mushrooms, cook slowly for 30 minutes.

MEAT BALLS, PROVINCIAL-STYLE   Serves 6

½ cup white bread cubes
¼ cup milk
1 pound ground beef
¼ pound sausage meat
1 cup minced onions
1 tablespoon minced parsley
½ teaspoon salt

¼ teaspoon black pepper
2 eggs
½ cup flour
¾ cup dry bread crumbs
vegetable oil for deep frying
parsley sprigs

- Soak bread cubes in the milk, mash.
- Combine next four ingredients with bread, salt, pepper and 1 egg; chill.
- Shape mixture into small balls; roll in flour, then in remaining beaten egg, then in bread crumbs.
- Fry meat balls at 375°F. until browned on all sides; drain and arrange on a hot serving dish.
- Garnish with fried parsley.

Variations:

CHILI MEAT BALLS

- Substitute ½ cup uncooked rice for milk and bread.
- Omit dipping in egg, flour and bread crumbs; brown in hot shortening.
- Add 2 cups tomato sauce, ¾ cup water, 1½ teaspoons chili powder and ½ teaspoon ground cumin seed.
- Cover and simmer 45 minutes.

Variations (continued)

GERMAN MEAT BALLS

- Add to meat mixture—

2 medium potatoes, cooked and mashed	2 anchovies, chopped

- Omit dipping in egg and bread crumbs.

- Add to browned meatballs, a mixture of—

3 tablespoons melted butter	1 tablespoon capers
2 tablespoons flour	1 tablespoon lemon juice
1 cup beef broth	

- Cover and simmer 20 - 25 minutes.

MEAT TURNOVERS   Serves 5

1 pound ground beef	nutmeg
¼ pound ground pork	¼ chopped walnuts
¼ cup seedless raisins	pie dough for 2 crust pie
cinnamon	1 egg yolk, diluted with water
cloves	

- Sauté beef and pork together for 15-20 minutes.

- Add next 5 ingredients, cook 5-10 minutes more. Roll out the pie dough and cut into 6 inch circles.

- Put a tablespoon of meat mixture in centre of each circle, fold over into a semi-circle.

- Mark edges and press together with the tines of a fork about ½ inch around the edge.

- Prick a few holes in the top of each.

- Brush the tops of each with an egg yolk diluted with a little water.

- Place on ungreased baking sheet, bake in 400°F. oven 15 minutes or until brown.

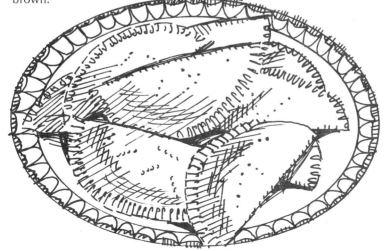

ORANGE-GLAZED MEAT LOAF   Serves 6 - 7

2 pounds ground beef	1 teaspoon salt
1½ .cups soft bread crumbs	½ cup fresh orange juice
1 egg	juice of 1 lemon
1 medium onion, minced	6 tablespoons brown sugar
1 medium green pepper, minced	½ teaspoon powdered mustard
¼ teaspoon pepper	6 slices of small orange, unpeeled

- Mix first 9 ingredients thoroughly.
- Place brown sugar in bottom of large loaf pan.
- Sprinkle with mustard and add orange slices.
- Press meat mixture into pan; bake in 350°F. oven for 1 hour; let stand 10 minutes before inverting onto heated platter.

Variation:

BEEF-TOMATO LOAF

- Substitute orange juice with milk; omit last 3 ingredients.
- Add to meat mixture, 1 tablespoon each horseradish, Worcestershire sauce and 1 cup canned tomatoes.
- Bake in 300°F. oven for 1½ hours; let stand 10 minutes before serving.

FARMER-STYLE LOAF

- Substitute ½ pound beef with sausage meat and bread crumbs with 2 potatoes finely chopped, orange juice with milk; omit last 3 ingredients.
- Add 1 apple finely diced and ½ cup chopped pimiento.
- Cover with foil and bake in 350°F. oven for 1½ hours; remove foil and bake 15 minutes longer.

BEEF 'N' OLIVE LOAF

- Substitute orange juice with milk and increase to 1½ cups; omit last 3 ingredients.
- Add to meat mixture, ½ cup chopped parsley, ½ cup shredded raw carrots, ½ cup chopped ripe olives, 1 clove garlic, minced, ½ teaspoon each sage, oregano.
- Bake in 350°F. oven for 1 hour.

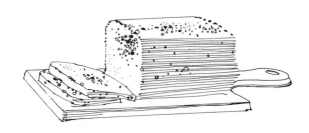

ORIENTAL HAMBURGERS   Serves 4

1 pound ground beef
¼ teaspoon black pepper
½ teaspoon ground ginger
½ teaspoon ground coriander

2 tablespoons soya sauce
½ cup chopped water chestnuts
2 tablespoons shortening

- Mix all ingredients except shortening; shape into 4 patties.
- Cook patties in hot shortening until desired degree of doneness; turn once.

HAMBURGERS RUSSIAN
- To meat add

¼ cup finely chopped onion,
  browned

salt, pepper
1½ cups sour cream

- Serve with mushroom sauce.

HAMBURGERS CALIFORNIA
- To meat add

1 ounce can devilled ham
  salt, pepper

½ cup dry red wine

MEXICAN CHEESE HAMBURGERS
- To meat add

¼ cup grated Parmesan cheese
1 cup chopped green onion
1 cup chopped parsley

1 egg
salt
cayenne pepper

HAMBURGERS HAWAIIAN
- To meat add

1 medium onion, chopped
1 clove garlic, minced

½ cup soya sauce
¼ teaspoon ground ginger

- Serve with pineapple slice.

HAMBURGER PIZZA
- Over cooked meat patties, pour pizza sauce, top with Mozzarella cheese and oregano; garnish with anchovy fillets and grated Parmesan cheese.
- Broil until hot.

PAPRIKA BURGERS
- To meat mixture add 2 tablespoons chopped onion.
- Make a sauce with

1 tablespoon butter or margarine
1 tablespoon flour
½ cup vegetable juice

1½ tablespoons paprika
1 teaspoon steak sauce

- Pour over burgers, cover and simmer 20 to 25 minutes.
- Place burgers on hot platter; stir 1 can cream of mushroom soup, 1 cup sour cream into sauce and serve with burgers over cooked noodles.

DANISH HAMBURGERS
- Cook hamburgers in butter with 1 cup sliced onion.

Variations (continued)

GIANT BURGERS

- Blend meat, salt, pepper and 1 clove garlic, minced.
- Shape into 2 large thin patties; place one in cake pan.
- Spread with ¼ cup prepared mustard and 2 cups thinly sliced onion; top with second pattie.
- Broil 4 minutes; cover and bake in 350°F. oven for 45 minutes.

BREADED FINNISH HAMBURGERS

- Prepare burgers with salt, pepper and chopped parsley.
- Dip in beaten egg then roll in dry bread crumbs before pan-frying.

PARSLIED STEAKS   Serves 6

6 frozen chopped beef steaks
3 tablespoons butter or margarine
4 green onions, trimmed and chopped
½ cup chopped parsley
½ teaspoon salt
½ teaspoon leaf marjoram, crumbled
¼ teaspoon pepper

- Sauté steaks on both sides in butter, remove to hot platter, overlapping steaks; keep warm while making sauce.
- Sauté green onions in drippings in pan until soft; stir in parsley, salt, majoram and pepper; heat until bubbling.
- Pour down centre of steaks.
- Serve with broccoli spears and pan browned or mashed potatoes.

PICNIC CHILI   Serves 4-5

1 pound ground beef, browned
20 ounce can beans with pork
1 teaspoon chili powder
½ cup diced green pepper
½ cup diced onion

- Mix all ingredients and simmer 15-20 minutes.

PIZZABURGER ITALIAN   Serves 6

2 tablespoons olive oil OR salad oil
½ cup chopped onion
1½ pounds ground beef
1 tablespoon minced parsley
½ teaspoon salt
¼ teaspoon black pepper
¼ teaspoon oregano
1 egg, beaten
6 English muffins, split and lightly toasted
1 cup tomato sauce, heated
12 slices Mozzarella or processed cheese

- Sauté onion 5 minutes, mix together the beef, parsley, salt, pepper, oregano and egg; add to onion and cook until browned, stir.
- Spread mixture on muffin halves; spread tomato sauce on each, then cover with a slice of cheese.
- Place under broiler until cheese melts.

SAUTEED BEEF BORDELAISE   Serves 4

1½ pounds ground beef
  1 envelope ground beef
    seasoning mix
  1 tablespoon dry red wine

¼ pound mushrooms, quartered
⅔ cup dry red wine
  1 10 ounce can beef gravy

- Combine ground beef, seasoning mix and 1 tablespoon dry red wine. Shape into 4 oval patties.
- Sauté patties 4 minutes on each side in a frying pan; remove.
- Sauté quartered mushrooms briefly in the same pan. Stir in dry red wine; simmer about 1 minute.
- Add canned beef gravy; heat to boiling. Return beef patties to pan 1 minute. Garnish with a watercress and sliced tomatoes.

STEAK TARTARE   Serves 4

1 pound filet of beef or
    sirloin steak, ground
½ cup finely chopped onion
1 clove garlic, minced
1 teaspoon salt

¾ teaspoon black pepper
3 tablespoons capers (optional)
5 egg yolks
    capers, chopped onion and
    minced parsley for garnish

- Mix meat, onion, garlic, salt, pepper, capers and 1 egg yolk.
- Shape lightly into 4 patties and make an indentation in each.
- Place a raw egg yolk in each, surround with capers, chopped onion and minced parsley.

STUFFED BURGERS   Serves 4

1 pound ground beef
1 medium onion, chopped
1 teaspoon salt
¼ teaspoon pepper
1⅓ cups soft bread crumbs

¼ teaspoon poultry seasoning
¼ teaspoon seasoned salt
¼ cup margarine or butter, melted
2 tablespoons lemon juice

- Mix beef, onion, salt and ⅛ teaspoon pepper; divide into 8 equal parts.
- Flatten each between pieces of wax paper until about 5 inches in diameter; leave on paper.
- Mix ⅛ teaspoon pepper and remaining ingredients; spread on 4 patties and top with remaining 4 patties.
- Crimp edges with a fork; remove from paper; broil until desired doneness, turn once.

Variation:

- Add relish or grated cheese to dressing.

STUFFED CABBAGE ROLLS   Serves 5

1 pound ground beef
½ cup uncooked rice
1 onion, minced
2 cloves garlic, minced
1 egg
　salt and pepper

1 white cabbage, cored
2 cups sauerkraut
3 cups canned tomatoes
1½ cups boiling water
3 tablespoons butter or margarine

- Mix first 7 ingredients.
- Put cabbage in boiling water over high heat; remove about 20 leaves as they wilt; let stand until warm only.
- Cut out coarse part of ribs; cool remaining cabbage and chop.
- Put half of chopped cabbage in a large kettle; put a spoonful of meat mixture in centre of each leaf; roll up, secure.
- Put on top of cabbage in kettle; top with remaining cabbage and remaining ingredients.
- Bring to boil, cover, simmer 45 minutes.

SURPRISE HAMBURGERS

With your 1 pound of lean ground beef, try mixing in one of the following:

1. A cup of grated Canadian Cheddar cheese, 1 clove garlic, minced, white wine, salt and pepper to taste.
2. A 5 ounce can of chopped water chestnuts, 2 chopped spring onions, 2 pinches of oregano and 2 tablespoons of soy sauce.
3. Three-quarters cup of finely chopped mushrooms, 3 pinches of marjoram, 1 tablespoon piccalilli, white wine, salt and pepper.
4. Three-quarters cup of grated carrot, 1 clove garlic, minced, 1 onion, chopped, 3 pinches of thyme, red wine, salt and pepper.
5. One-quarter cup tomato paste, diluted with ½ cup of tomato juice, ¼ teaspoon sugar, 1 tablespoon chopped dill pickle, salt and pepper.
6. Three-quarters cup of finely chopped walnuts, ½ teaspoon of fresh or dried dill seed, red wine.
7. One-half cup of grated tart apple, one chopped green onion, ⅓ cup of toasted chopped almonds, red wine.

TOMATO STEAK PIE

Serves 4 - 5

1½ pounds ground beef
  1 onion, sliced
  6 tomato slices

1 cup catsup
1 tablespoon Worcestershire sauce
¼ cup water

- Pat beef into deep 9-inch pie plate; top with onion and tomato slices.
- Mix remaining ingredients; pour over meat.
- Bake in 400°F. oven for 30 minutes; pour off some of the fat.
- Cut into wedges.

WESTERN-STYLE CHILI CON CARNE

Serves 6

  2 tablespoons vegetable oil
1½ cups thinly sliced onions
  1 cup chopped green pepper
1½ pounds boneless beef,
    cut in cubes
  3 cups canned tomatoes

1 teaspoon salt
½ teaspoon black pepper
2 tablespoons chili powder
1 clove garlic, minced
2 cups red kidney beans

- Sauté onions and green pepper in hot oil 10 minutes.
- Add meat and brown over medium heat, stirring frequently.
- Mix in tomatoes, salt, pepper, chili powder and garlic; cover and cook over low heat 2 hours.
- Add beans, cook 10 minutes longer.

ZINGY HASH

Serves 6

1 pound ground beef
3 large onions, sliced
1 large green pepper, chopped
1 16 ounce can tomatoes

½ cup uncooked rice
1½ teaspoons salt
1½ teaspoons chili powder
⅛ teaspoon pepper

- In large frying pan cook and stir meat, onion and green pepper until meat is brown and vegetables are tender.
- Drain off fat.
- Stir in tomatoes, rice, salt, chili powder and pepper.
- Heat through.
- Pour into a 2 quart ungreased casserole and bake covered in 350°F. oven for 1 hour.

$\approx$VEAL SECTION$\approx$

VEAL AND SHELLS PLATTER   Serves 6

1 8 ounce package maruzzelle
  (small shells), or elbow macaroni
1 pound frozen veal patties
4 tablespoons butter or margarine

¼ cup vegetable oil
1 large onion, chopped
1 clove of garlic, minced
1 cup chopped parsley

- Cook shells in a kettle, follow label directions; drain; return to kettle.
- While shells cook, combine butter and oil in a large frying pan until foamy.
- Add onion and garlic; sauté until soft; stir in parsley, cook 1 minute.
- Remove onion with slotted spoon; add to drained shells.
- Pour half the butter mixture over shells, tossing until evenly coated.
- Cut veal patties in half. Brown, turning once, in oil remaining in pan.
- Pile shells into center of a heated platter and arrange veal around.
- Drizzle drippings in pan over veal. Serve with grated Parmesan cheese.

VEAL BALLS IN TOMATO SAUCE   Serves 6

1½ pounds ground lean veal
  2 eggs, beaten
  1 tablespoon Marsala or sweet sherry
  ½ cup grated Parmesan cheese
  2 teaspoons salt
  ½ teaspoon black pepper

¼ cup flour
4 tablespoons butter or margarine
½ cup chopped onion
1 clove garlic, minced
3 cups canned tomatoes
2 tablespoons minced parsley

- Mix together the veal, eggs, wine, cheese and half the salt and pepper; shape into 1 inch balls and roll lightly in flour.
- Sauté the onion in butter 10 minutes; add garlic, tomatoes and remaining salt and pepper.
- Bring to a boil and cook over low heat 20 minutes; add meat balls; cover and cook over low heat 1 hour; sprinkle with parsley.
- Serve with rice or noodles.

Variation:

STROGANOFF-STYLE VEAL BALLS

- Add to meat mixture ½ cup light cream and ½ cup grated, drained potatoes.
- Sauté 1 cup sliced mushrooms with onion.
- Substitute 1 cup beef broth for tomatoes.
- During last 5 minutes, stir in 1 cup sour cream and ½ teaspoon paprika.
- Serve with noodles or dumplings.

VEAL BIRDS   Serves 6

½ pound ground veal	½ teaspoon black pepper
1 clove garlic, minced	1½ pounds veal cutlet, cut
¼ cup finely chopped parsley	into 6 pieces and pounded thin
2 tablespoons dry white wine	⅓ cup flour
⅛ teaspoon nutmeg	6 tablespoons butter
1 teaspoon salt	¼ teaspoon sage

- Mix together first 6 ingredients with ½ teaspoon of the salt and ¼ teaspoon of the pepper.
- Spread some of the mixture on each of the cutlets, roll up, tie with thread.
- Mix flour with remaining salt and pepper; dip the rolls in the mixture.
- Melt the butter in a frying pan; add sage and rolls; sauté over medium heat 20 minutes or until brown on all sides and tender.
- Remove threads before serving.

VEAL CROQUETTES WITH CREAM SAUCE   Serves 4

1 cup white bread cubes	¼ cup minced parsley
½ cup light cream	½ cup flour
1 pound ground lean veal	3 tablespoons vegetable oil
1 teaspoon salt	2 tablespoons butter or margarine
½ teaspoon white pepper	½ cup dry white wine
⅛ teaspoon nutmeg	½ teaspoon marjoram
1 egg, beaten	½ cup cream

- Soak the bread until very soft in light cream, then mash smooth.
- Mix with next 5 ingredients and 3 tablespoons of the parsley; shape into 8 croquettes; dip in the flour.
- Brown the croquettes in hot oil on all sides; pour off most of the fat; cover and cook over low heat 15 minutes, turning once.
- Transfer croquettes to a hot serving platter; pour off the fat; add wine and marjoram; bring to a boil.
- Add cream; cook over high heat 3 minutes; stir in small pieces of the remaining butter until melted.
- Pour over the patties and sprinkle with the remaining parsley.

VEAL DUMPLINGS   Serves 4

1 pound ground lean veal
¼ pound cooked ham, finely chopped
4 tablespoons grated Parmesan cheese
2 eggs, beaten
2 teaspoons salt

1 cup dry bread crumbs
4 tablespoons butter or margarine
4 tablespoons dry vermouth
1 pound tomatoes, chopped
¼ teaspoon black pepper

- Mix together the veal, ham, cheese, eggs and 1 teaspoon of salt; shape tablespoons of the mixture into little balls; roll in the bread crumbs.
- Brown balls on all sides in melted butter; add wine; cook until absorbed; add tomatoes, pepper and remaining salt; cook over low heat 30 minutes.
- Serve with steamed rice or noodles and a bowl of grated cheese.

VEAL LOAF   Serves 6

2 pounds ground veal
1 green pepper, finely chopped
1 clove garlic, mashed
1 pound ground ham

2 medium onions, chopped
2 teaspoons salt
2 eggs

- Mix ingredients until they are completely and smoothly blended; form into a loaf and place in a baking pan or on a rack in the pan.
- Cover top with a few strips of bacon or salt pork; bake in a 350°F. oven 1 to 1½ hours; baste with drippings in the pan once or twice during cooking.
- Serve hot or cold.

Variations:

With Olives: Instead of green pepper, add 10 or 12 sliced stuffed olives.
With Mushrooms: Add, instead of green pepper, 1 cup finely chopped mushrooms and proceed as above.
With Sour Cream: Use one egg and add ½ cup sour cream and ⅛ teaspoon nutmeg. Serve over creamed spinach and potato balls.

VEAL MOUSSE   Serves 8

2 pounds ground lean veal
1 teaspoon salt
½ teaspoon white pepper

3 egg whites
1½ cups light cream

- Beat the salt, pepper and unbeaten egg whites into meat; gradually beat in cream.
- Turn the mixture into a well-greased 8-inch ring mold; cover with a piece of greased waxed paper or foil and place in a pan containing 1-inch boiling water.
- Bake in a 350°F. oven 45 minutes or until set.
- Remove from oven and let stand 5 minutes; turn out onto a heated serving dish; serve with hollandaise, mushroom or tomato sauce.

158

PORK SECTION

BAKED HAM AND PORK BALLS

Serves 4

¾ pound ground, cooked ham
½ pound lean pork, ground
½ cup milk
½ cup cracker crumbs
¾ cup brown sugar, packed

½ cup vinegar
½ cup water
6 whole cloves
1 tablespoon powdered mustard

- Mix first 4 ingredients and shape into 12 2 inch balls.
- Place in shallow baking dish.
- Bring remaining ingredients to boil; pour over ham balls; bake uncovered in 325°F. oven for 2 hours.

BRAISED PORK IN SOY SAUCE

Serves 6

1½ pounds pork, cut in small cubes
2 tablespoons cooking oil
1 large onion, sliced
2 green peppers, sliced
2 cloves garlic, minced

1 teaspoon ground ginger
¼ cup soya sauce
1 tablespoon brown sugar
½ cup water
¼ cup sliced mushrooms

- Pan fry meat in very hot oil until lightly browned; add next 4 ingredients; reduce heat and sauté for 5 minutes.
- Add rest of ingredients and simmer for 40 minutes.

CURRIED PORK

Serves 6

½ cup all-purpose flour
  salt and pepper
½ teaspoon ground ginger
2 pounds lean pork, cut into
  1 inch cubes
¼ cup butter or margarine

1 tablespoon curry powder
⅛ teaspoon chili powder
1 cup chopped onion
¾ cup chopped green pepper
2 cups hot bouillon

- Coat pork in mixture of first four ingredients; brown on all sides in butter, stir in curry and chili powder.
- Add remaining ingredients; cover and simmer 1¼ to 1½ hours or until pork is tender, stir occasionally.

GOURMET SAUSAGE AND NOODLES   Serves 6

1 pound bulk pork sausage,
   formed into patties
2 cups fine noodles, cooked
2 tablespoons chopped pimiento
2 tablespoons chopped green pepper
¼ cup milk

1 can condensed cream of chicken soup
½ cup crumbled blue cheese
½ cup soft bread crumbs
1 tablespoon melted butter or
   margarine

- Brown sausage patties lightly on both sides; drain.
- Combine patties, noodles, pimiento and green pepper.
- Add milk to soup; heat, stirring constantly, add blue cheese; heat, stir until cheese melts.
- Combine sauce with noodle mixture.
- Turn into greased 2-quart casserole; top with buttered crumbs.
- Bake in 350°F. oven 30 to 35 minutes.

HAM AND SAUSAGE LOAF   Serves 6

1 cup seasoned bread stuffing mix
¾ cup boiling water
1 cup cream-style corn
1 egg

½ cup chopped parsley
1 pound bulk sausage
¼ cup dark corn syrup
4 cups finely chopped cooked ham

- Combine bread stuffing mix with boiling water in a large bowl; add corn, egg, add parsley, ham and sausage; mix lightly until well-blended.
- Moisten a 6 cup oven mold or bowl and pack meat mixture firmly into mold; invert loaf onto shallow baking pan.
- Bake in 350°F. oven 1 hour and 15 minutes. Brush loaf with syrup and bake 15 minutes longer, or until loaf is well-glazed.
- Serve on platter garnished with pepper squash and buttered asparagus.

PORK CHOP SUEY   Serves 4

½ pound lean pork (shoulder),
   cubed
2 tablespoons fat
3 cups beef stock OR
3 cups water and 3 bouillon cubes
1 cup sliced mushrooms
1½ cups thinly sliced celery

½ cup chopped celery leaves
1 cup sliced onion
⅔ cup sliced green pepper
1 teaspoon salt
¾ teaspoon Worcestershire sauce
3 tablespoons quick-cooking tapioca

- Brown pork in fat; add half of stock and continue cooking until meat is tender.
- Add remaining stock, vegetables and seasonings; cover and simmer until vegetables are tender but still crisp.
- Drain off stock, measure and add water to make 2¼ cups. Add stock and tapioca to meat mixture and cook over low or medium heat until mixture comes to a boil, stirring constantly; serve hot with rice.

PORK-STUFFED CABBAGE ROLLS   Serves 5 - 6

1 large head green cabbage
2 tablespoons shortening
1 cup finely chopped onion
¼ teaspoon finely chopped garlic
1 pound ground lean pork
¾ cup cooked rice
2 eggs, lightly beaten

2 tablespoons paprika
⅛ teaspoon marjoram
1 teaspoon salt
black pepper
4 cups canned sauerkraut, drained
1 cup water mixed, with
1 cup tomato purée

SAUCE:
3 tablespoons unsalted butter
2 tablespoons flour
1 cup sour cream

- Simmer cabbage in boiling salted water for 8 to 10 minutes, remove, drain, cool.
- Remove unbroken large outer leaves, towel dry, set aside.
- Sauté onion and garlic in hot fat until lightly coloured.
- Combine next 7 ingredients; add onion mixture.
- Place 2 tablespoons of meat mixture in centre of each wilted cabbage leaf; roll up tightly, secure.
- Spread sauerkraut on bottom of large casserole; top with cabbage rolls and tomato sauce.
- Cover and simmer for 1 hour.
- Mix sauce ingredients together; heat; stir into sauerkraut mixture; serve with cabbage rolls.

PORK-STUFFED ORANGES ORIENTAL   Serves 8

8 large oranges
2 tablespoons vegetable oil
1 tablespoon minced garlic
1½ pounds ground lean pork
¼ cup chopped peanuts
¼ teaspoon ground coriander

½ teaspoon dried ground
chili peppers
2 teaspoons soya sauce
2 tablespoons dry sherry
¾ teaspoon salt
1 cup water

- Wash the unpeeled oranges and make four cuts in each running from the top to within ½ inch of the bottom, spread oranges open, remove the pits.
- Sauté garlic in oil 2 minutes; add remaining ingredients and cook 15 to 20 minutes.
- Fill orange centres; place on rack in casserole, add water.
- Bake in 350°F. oven for 15 minutes.

⇝ LAMB SECTION ⇜

LAMB LOAF   Serves 4

2 pounds ground lamb	1 teaspoon salt
1 cup dry bread crumbs	1 teaspoon dry mustard
¼ cup finely chopped onion	2 eggs
¼ cup finely chopped parsley	bacon strips
1 clove garlic, finely chopped	

- Mix together first 7 ingredients; form into a loaf; top with bacon strips.
- Bake in a 350°F. oven for approximately 1 hour.
- Serve with French fried onion rings and a green salad.

LAMB PATTIES

- Lamb patties are ground lamb formed into cakes and usually wrapped with bacon secured with small skewers. They may be broiled in the same manner as lamb chops, but should be lubricated well with butter or oil during the cooking process. Lamb patties should not be over-cooked.

LAMB STUFFED CABBAGE   Serves 6

1 pound cooked lamb, ground	⅛ teaspoon pepper
2 cups cooked rice	1 15 ounce can tomato sauce
1 egg	1 head of cabbage (about 3½ pounds)
1 clove garlic, crushed	2 tablespoons butter or margarine
¾ teaspoon salt	1 cup chopped onion
¼ teaspoon leaf thyme, crumbled	2 teaspoons sugar
⅓ teaspoon leaf rosemary, crumbled	¼ teaspoon salt
	½ cup water

- Combine first 8 ingredients and ⅔ cup of the tomato sauce, mix well.
- Trim outside leaves from cabbage.
- Cut a small slice about 3 inches in diameter from top end; set aside.
- Hollow out cabbage, leaving a shell about ½ inch thick. (Chop cut-out pieces coarsely and cook separately to serve with stuffed cabbage or save to cook as a vegetable for another day.)
- Spoon lamb mixture into shell, pressing it down firmly, fit top back into place; tie with a string.
- Sauté onion in hot butter until soft, about 5 minutes; add remaining tomato sauce, sugar, salt and water.
- Bring to boiling, stir constantly. Remove from heat.
- Place cabbage, core end down, in a deep casserole or Dutch oven; pour sauce over; cover.
- Bake in 350°F. oven for 1 hour and 30 minutes, baste several times.
- Place stuffed cabbage on a heated serving platter; remove string.
- Spoon some of sauce over cabbage; cut into wedges.

⇨POULTRY SECTION⇦

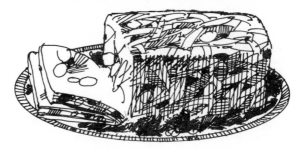

CHICKEN AND ALMOND LOAF WITH MUSHROOM SAUCE
Serves 4

3 cups chopped cooked chicken
½ cup blanched almonds,
  coarsely chopped or slivered
2 tablespoon finely chopped onion,
  sautéed in butter or margarine
1 cup milk

1 cup soft breadcrumbs
2 eggs
¾ cup celery, chopped
1 cup chicken stock
  salt and pepper

- Mix ingredients, in the order given.
- Bake in buttered bread pan in 375°F. oven 45 minutes. Serve in slices with mushroom sauce or giblet gravy.

Mushroom Sauce

1 10-ounce can cream of mushroom
  soup

2 tablespoons sherry
1 teaspoon lemon juice

- Mix ingredients together; heat and serve with sliced chicken loaf.

CHICKEN CHOW MEIN
Serves 4

2 tablespoons corn oil
3 medium onions, chopped
1 cup sliced mushrooms
3 cups chopped celery
2 cups chicken broth
2 teaspoons soy sauce

2 teaspoons cornstarch
  water
2 cups diced cooked chicken
1 cup bean sprouts
4 cups cooked rice

- Heat oil in wok or skillet, stir fry or sauté onions until golden; add mushrooms and celery; stir fry briefly.
- Stir in broth and soy sauce; bring to boil.
- Mix cornstarch with a little water until smooth; whisk into onion mixture; add chicken and sprouts. (Reheat but do not boil.)
- Serve over rice.

CHICKEN' HAM JAMBALAYA   Serves 8

2 2 pound broiler-fryers, cut up
1 cup diced, cooked ham
3 tablespoons butter or margarine
1 clove garlic, minced
2 cups chopped onion

4 cups stewed or canned tomatoes
1 teaspoon salt
½ teaspoon chili powder
1 cup uncooked rice
2 cups sliced celery

- Brown chicken pieces lightly in butter in Dutch oven; remove chicken pieces, brown ham lightly.
- Add garlic and onions, sauté 5 minutes, return chicken.
- Add tomatoes, salt and chili powder to chicken mixture, bring to boiling, lower heat, simmer, covered 30 minutes.
- Add rice and celery, cook 30 minutes longer or until chicken and rice are tender.

CHICKEN, MUSHROOM AND BACON RICE   Serves 4

3 cups diced cooked chicken
10 ounce can condensed cream of
   mushroom soup
½ cup light cream

2 tablespoons sherry
Tarragon
Lemon peel

Bacon Rice

1½ cups raw rice
3 cups chicken broth or chicken
   bouillon cubes and 3 cups water

3 green onions, tops and bottoms
   chopped
4 slices bacon, cooked crumbled

- Heat the chicken in mushroom soup with the cream and sherry.
- Add a pinch only of tarragon and a pinch only of grated lemon peel.
- Put rice in pan with the chicken broth and onions, bring to a boil, cover, and turn the heat down very low for 15-20 minutes.
- Remove lid, fluff rice with a fork.
- Add the crumbled cooked bacon, put into a serving dish.

CHICKEN'N ALMONDS   Serves 4

2 tablespoons cooking oil
1 teaspoon salt
2 cups diced cooked chicken
1 cup diced celery
⅓ cup sliced water chestnuts

1 cup frozen peas
½ cup bamboo shoots
2 tablespoons cornstarch
   mixed with ½ cup cold water
½ cup slivered almonds

- Put the oil in a hot frying pan, add salt and chicken, stir well.
- Add celery, water chestnuts, peas and bamboo shoots.
- Add 1 cup water, cover, cook 10 minutes.
- Add cornstarch mixture, stir, and sprinkle with the almonds.

CHICKEN SUPREME PUFF   Serves 6

1 can condensed cream of
  chicken soup
1 cup milk
2 cups cooked chicken, cubed
2½ tablespoons butter or
  margarine

¼ cup flour
¾ cup milk
4 eggs, separated
¾ teaspoon salt
4 drops Tabasco sauce
¼ teaspoon cream of tartar

- Blend soup with 1 cup milk. Combine with chicken in 2 quart casserole.
- Melt butter in small saucepan, blend in flour; cook, stirring constantly, until bubbly; stir in ¾ cup milk, continue cooking and stirring until mixture thickens and bubbles 1 minute; cool.
- Beat yolks with salt and Tabasco sauce in a large bowl. Beat in hot mixture.
- Beat whites with cream of tartar until stiff peaks form. Fold whites, add ½ at a time, into yolk mixture only until well combined. Spoon soufflé mixture over chicken in baking dish.
- Bake in 375°F. oven 40 minutes, or until puffed and browned.

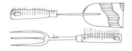

CHICKEN WITH ORANGE AND ALMONDS   Serves 4

4 tablespoons butter or margarine
2 cups rice
1 barbecued chicken, meat removed
  from the bones and cut in serving
  pieces

4 cups chicken broth
¼ cup slivered almonds
2 tablespoons chopped candied
  orange peel

- Cook rice in butter over low heat until opaque.
- Add chicken, chicken broth and orange peel.
- Bring rice and chicken mixture to a boil, cover, turn heat down, simmer about 35 minutes.
- Remove lid, stir in almonds, fluff with a fork.

POULTRY SHORTCAKE   Serves 4

2 cups diced cooked chicken,
  turkey or duck
¼ pound sliced fresh mushrooms
3 tablespoons butter
3 tablespoons flour

1 cup chicken broth
½ cup sour cream
2 tablespoons sherry
4 toasted English muffins

- Sauté mushrooms in butter, remove and sprinkle with flour, cook until almost dry.
- Add broth, a little at a time, stirring constantly until smooth and thickened.
- Add cream and cook until thickened. Do not boil. Add sherry, diced chicken, cooked mushrooms.
- Mix and pour between and on top of the split and toasted muffin halves.

QUICK CHICKEN CREOLE   Serves 4

3 cups hot cooked rice
2 tablespoons butter or margarine
½ cup chopped green pepper
1 medium size onion, chopped
½ cup thinly sliced celery
1 clove of garlic, mashed
1 can condensed chicken rice soup

2 cups canned tomatoes
1 3-4 ounce can sliced mushrooms, drained
2 cups cooked chicken, diced
¼ teaspoon leaf marjoram, crumbled
¼ teaspoon salt
1 cup shredded process cheese

- Place cooked rice in a lightly greased 2 quart casserole.
- Sauté green pepper, onion, celery and garlic in butter until tender.
- Stir in remaining ingredients, except cheese.
- Pour mixture over rice, spreading evenly; sprinkle with cheese; cover.
- Bake in 350°F. oven 30 minutes, or until bubbly-hot.

TURKEY CASSEROLE   Serves 4

½ pound mushrooms, sliced
1 onion, minced
3 tablespoons butter or margarine
4 tablespoons flour
salt and pepper
10 ounce can chicken noodle soup

½ cup half cream, half milk
⅓ cup white wine
3 cups diced cooked turkey
1 small jar chopped pimientos
½ cup chopped ripe olives
2 cups Chinese noodles

- Sauté mushrooms and the onions in butter until lightly browned.
- Sprinkle flour on top; add salt and pepper, stir until blended.
- Gradually add the half-and-half, soup mix, stir until thickened and smooth.
- Add white wine, stir until blended, then add the turkey, pimientos, and ripe olives.
- Mix together and pour over the noodles in a shallow casserole. Heat and serve.

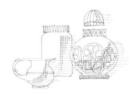

TURKEY HASH   Serves 8

3 tablespoons butter or margarine
4 tablespoons flour
2 cups light cream

salt and pepper
2 cups diced cooked turkey
2 tablespoons sherry

- Make a cream sauce by melting butter, adding flour, and cooking slightly before adding the cream slowly.
- Stir constantly while cooking over low heat, until smooth and thickened.
- Add salt and pepper, turkey and sherry. Heat thoroughly. (This may be made ahead of time and kept warm in a double boiler.)
- Serve on a rice ring cooked in cranberry juice and season with ginger.

HAWAIIAN WIENERS

Serves 6

3 tablespoons butter or margarine
1 large onion, chopped
1 green pepper, slivered
1 cup cubed canned pineapple,
   drained
2 small tomatoes, peeled and chopped
2 tablespoons cornstarch

½ cup pineapple juice
1 tablespoon white vinegar
1 pound wieners, cut into
   2 inch pieces
   salt and pepper
   hot cooked rice

- Sauté onion, green pepper, pineapple and tomatoes in butter for 7 minutes.
- Blend next three ingredients and stir into vegetables.
- Add wieners, salt and pepper; simmer, covered, for about 10 minutes, stir frequently.
- Serve with hot cooked rice.

MEATY RISI PISI

Serves 4

¼ cup onions, finely chopped
2 tablespoons butter or margarine
1½ cups long grain rice
1 tablespoon dry white wine
3 cups hot beef consommé
1 cup fresh or frozen cooked peas
1½ cups diced cooked ham,
   tongue, or lamb

⅓ cup freshly grated Parmesan
   or Romano cheese
1 small jar pimientos, diced
⅓ cup finely chopped parsley
   salt and pepper

- Cook onions in the butter until lightly coloured, add rice and stir in butter and onion mixture until opaque.
- Add consommé and wine, bring to a boil, cover, turn heat down very low.
- Cook 15-20 minutes, remove from heat, fluff with a fork, add peas, ham, cheese, pimientos, and parsley.
- Season to taste.

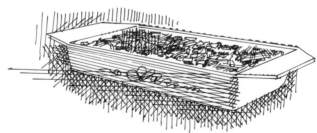

OLD FASHIONED HASH

Serves 4

1 small onion, chopped
2 tablespoons butter or margarine
1½ cups diced cooked meat, beef,
   lamb, or pork

2 cups diced, cooked potatoes
⅓ cup catsup
1 finely chopped dill pickle

- Sauté onion in butter, add meat and potatoes; brown slightly, stir well.
- Stir in the catsup, heat thoroughly.
- Before serving, sprinkle top with chopped dill pickle.

FISH
FOR
ECONOMY

FISH FOR ECONOMY

All too often fish and seafood are considered meat substitute rather than a permanent part of any weekly menu. Let's look at the one area that makes people shy away from this versatile food.

Questions like — How to buy fish?
How much to buy?
What kind, what form?

The following suggestion should help to answer these questions. Since fish adapts so beautifully to all kinds of seasoning, the possibilities for recipes are almost endless.

Fish is adaptable too, it is great fried, broiled, baked, poached or steamed.

What more would anyone ask except to learn that fish is also a money saver.

FROZEN FISH

May be bought by the pound, whole, dressed, in steaks, fillets, chunks, portions and sticks. Throughout the year you'll see numerous varieties available.

- Look for the following characteristics as a guide to buying frozen fish of good quality: The flesh should be solidly frozen when you buy it and should not be discolored or have any freezer burn. It should have little or no odor.
- Keep frozen (at 0°F.) until ready to use. Store in its original wrapper. Follow label directions for thawing and cooking.

CANNED FISH

Comes in a wide variety of styles and often offers an economical alternative to fresh or frozen fish. Tuna, salmon, crab and sardines are the most abundant kinds of canned fish.

GOOD FISH BUYS

Consider the less expensive kinds of fish: Turbot, cod, red snapper, pollock, flounder and haddock — instead of trout, halibut and sole. Also, whiting and ocean perch offer good value.

- Buy frozen fish rather than fresh, unless you live in a fishing area where prices are extremely good. And if you're willing to fillet any fish, you'll save about 50 percent.
- Remember that all white meat fillets can be interchanged in recipes if breaded, rolled, stuffed or topped with sauce. So choose the least expensive for such recipes.

STORAGE

- Fresh fish will keep in the refrigerator (at 35°F. to 40°F.) for one to two days before cooking.
- Frozen raw fish can be kept in the freezer (at 0°F.) in its original wrapper, up to six months.
- Cooked fish products can be stored in the refrigerator for three to four days and in the freezer for about three months.
- Canned fish should be stored in a cool, dry place for no more than a year.

HOW MUCH TO BUY PER SERVING

As a general guide, keep these amounts in mind when purchasing fish:

Whole	¾ to 1 pound
Dressed or Pan-Dressed	½ pound
Fillets or Steaks	⅓ pound
Sticks	¼ pound
Portions	⅓ pound
Canned	1/6 pound

BASS AND SAUSAGE

- For a novelty, stuff bass with sausage meat, and grill over the coals.

CLAM CHOWDER   Serves 6-8

3 slices bacon, chopped, cooked crisp
1 cup chopped onion
4 medium-size potatoes, pared
  and diced
3 cups water
½ teaspoon salt

¼ teaspoon pepper
2 10 ounce cans clams, chopped
1 cup clam juice
4 tablespoons instant nonfat dry milk
3 tablespoons flour
2 tablespoons minced parsley

- Add onion to bacon drippings, sauté until soft.
- Add potatoes, 2 cups of the water, salt and pepper; cover; simmer 15 minutes, or until potatoes are tender. Remove from heat.
- Drain liquid from clams into a 4 cup measure; reserve clams. Add 1 cup clam juice and remaining cup of water.
- Combine dry milk with flour in a small bowl; stir briskly into clam liquids in cup. Add to potato mixture in saucepan. Cook, stirring constantly, over medium heat, until chowder thickens and bubbles 1 minute.
- Add clams; heat just until piping-hot. Ladle into soup bowls.
- Sprinkle with parsley and reserved bacon. Serve with crackers.

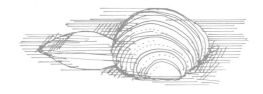

TOP OF STOVE COD SUPPER   Serves 4

1 cup chopped onion
1 clove of garlic, minced
3 tablespoons olive oil or
  vegetable oil
2 large ripe tomatoes, peeled,
  cored, chopped
¾ teaspoon salt

1 teaspoon leaf thyme, crumbled
¼ teaspoon pepper
1 pound frozen cod fillets
  (not thawed)
  boiled potatoes
  cucumber slices
  chopped parsley

- Sauté onion and garlic in a large frying pan in oil until soft.
- Stir tomatoes into onion mixture, cook 2 minutes; add salt, thyme and pepper.
- Place frozen fish block in the sauce spooning part of the sauce over fish; cover.
- Simmer 20 minutes, or until fish flakes easily with a fork. Transfer fish to a heated serving platter; spoon sauce over and around fish. Surround with boiled potatoes and cucumber slices; garnish with chopped parsley.

CRAB PILAF

Serves 4

1 pound crabmeat
4 strips of bacon
2 onions, finely chopped
1 clove garlic, chopped fine
1 cup raw rice
2 cups white wine

¼ cup cognac
¼ cup chopped parsley
2 tomatoes, peeled, seeded,
and chopped
salt
⅓ cup heavy or sour cream

- Sauté bacon in a heavy cold frying pan, heat slowly until crisp. Remove bacon.
- Add onion, garlic, and rice to the bacon fat.
- Cook until onion is transparent and also the rice.
- Add wine, parsley, bring to a boil, cover, turn heat down low, cook for 15-20 minutes or until liquid is absorbed. Stir in cognac, chopped tomato, crabmeat, bacon, cook until hot.
- Stir in cream just before serving.

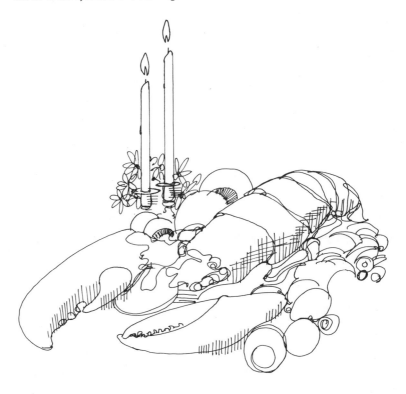

CRAB CREPES WITH MORNAY SAUCE

Crabmeat Mixture

1 pound fresh crabmeat
1 teaspoon onion finely chopped
⅓ cup heavy cream
6 tablespoons butter or margarine

6 ounces white wine
1 teaspoon Dijon mustard
salt and pepper

- Melt butter; add the finely chopped onion and white wine. Cook slowly until reduced to about half the quantity.

- Add the heavy cream, mustard, salt and pepper to the crabmeat which has been carefully picked apart to remove the thin membranes. Cook over a low flame 10 minutes.

Thin pancakes

¾ cup cake flour, sifted
1 tablespoon icing sugar
2 tablespoons melted butter or margarine

2 eggs plus 2 egg yolks
1¾ cups milk
1 teaspoon cognac or rum
salt

- Sift flour, sugar and a pinch of salt.

- Beat eggs and mix with dry ingredients.

- Add milk slowly, stir until smooth. Add melted butter and liquor. Strain through a fine sieve.

- Make the batter at least 2 hours before using. To bake the cakes, put a little batter in a very hot frying or crêpe pan. Pour in a thin layer of batter, cook until brown on one side, turn over and brown on other side. Cook quickly — long cooking toughens them.

Mornay Sauce

2 tablespoons butter or margarine
3 tablespoons flour
2 cups milk
¼ teaspoon salt

¼ cup coarsely grated Swiss cheese
nutmeg
salt and pepper

- Melt butter in saucepan over low heat, blend in the flour, and cook slowly, stirring, until ingredients froth together for 2 minutes without colouring.

- Remove from heat and, as soon as *roux* has stopped bubbling, pour in the milk and salt, which have been heated to a boil.

- Immediately beat vigorously with a wire whip to blend, gathering all bits of *roux* from the inside edges of the pan.

- Set saucepan over moderately high heat and stir with the wire whip until béchamel comes to a boil. Boil for 1 minute, stirring.

- Then remove from heat and beat in the cheese until it has melted and blended with the sauce. Season to taste with salt, pepper, and a pinch of nutmeg.

- Put some of crabmeat mixture on each pancake, roll up, and place side by side in a buttered baking dish.

- Cover with Mornay Sauce and brown in a medium oven 10 minutes or until brown and bubbly.

FLOUNDER FILLETS GARNI   Serves 6

2 1 pound packages frozen flounder
  fillets, thawed
¼ cup butter or margarine
2 tablespoons lemon juice
1 teaspoon paprika

mashed potatoes
2 cups frozen mixed vegetables,
  cooked, drained, and seasoned
2 tomatoes, cut in halves
Watercress

- Separate fish fillets carefully; arrange in a single layer on a cooky sheet.
- Melt butter in a small saucepan; stir in lemon juice and paprika.
- Brush part of mixture on fish fillets.
- Broil fillets about 4 inches from heat about 5 minutes.
- Transfer fillets from cooky sheet with wide spatula, layering in the centre of a seasoned 15 x 10 inch wooden or flameproof platter.
- Fill a pastry bag with mashed potatoes; pipe 6 nests of potatoes around the plank; border plank between nests with remaining potatoes. Brush remaining paprika-butter on fish.
- Bake in 400°F. oven 15 minutes, or until potatoes are tipped with golden-brown.
- At serving time, fill potato nests with seasoned mixed vegetables.
- Garnish plank with broiled tomato halves and watercress.

TARRAGON BROILED LOBSTER TAILS   Serves 4

4 frozen lobster tails
3 tablespoons tarragon vinegar,
  with the tarragon leaves in it or
1 teaspoon dried tarragon

¼ cup butter or margarine
1 tablespoon chopped chives
½ teaspoon dry mustard
  salt and pepper

- Remove with scissors the soft part of the lobster tail and slightly hit the hard upper shell with a mallet or cleaver so that it will lie flat.
- Melt the butter, add the vinegar, chives and seasonings. Spoon generously over the lobster tails and let stand in marinade for several hours.
- Broil about 10-15 minutes with meaty side up, basting from time to time, with the liquid in the pan. Broil about 4 inches from heat.

LOBSTER

- Kill lobster by inserting knife in back between body and tail shells. Split lengthwise and clean. Wash and dry carefully. Brush meat with melted butter or oil. Dust with salt and pepper.
- Broil (shell side down) until shell browns. Turn over and brown meaty side. Baste frequently with butter or oil. Serve with melted butter and lemon juice.

INDIVIDUAL SALMON FLORENTINE SHELLS   Serves 4

1 package frozen spinach   2 tablespoons flour
 (about 10 ounces),   ½ teaspoon salt
 thawed, chopped   ½ teaspoon dillweed
1 pound can, drained pink   1¼ cups milk
 salmon   1 egg, beaten
2 tablespoons butter or margarine 2 tablespoons lemon juice

- Remove skin and bones from salmon; break into small pieces.
- Melt butter in a small saucepan; stir in flour, salt and dillweed.
- Cook, stir constantly, until bubbly; stir in milk; continue cooking and stirring until sauce thickens and bubbles 1 minute.
- Stir half of hot mixture into beaten egg; return to saucepan; cook, stirring constantly, 1 minute, or until sauce thickens again.
- Stir in lemon juice.
- Fold 1 cup of the hot sauce into salmon.
- Line 4 scallop shells or 4 individual foil baking dishes with chopped spinach.
- Spoon salmon mixture onto center of spinach, spoon remaining hot sauce over salmon.
- Broil 3 minutes (about 4 inches from heat) or until tops are light brown and bubbly. Garnish with a slice of lemon and a sprig of parsley.

MARINATED SALMON STEAKS   Serves 4

4 fresh or frozen salmon steaks ¼ teaspoon dill weed
 (about 1 inch thick)   ½ teaspoon dry mustard
⅓ cup white table wine   1 lemon, thinly sliced, seeds removed
⅓ cup olive or salad oil

- Arrange salmon steaks in a shallow baking dish, mix seasonings together, pour over steaks.
- Arrange lemon slices on top.
- Let stand in juices 3-4 hours. Remove from the marinade, place fish steaks on a greased broiler rack, broil carefully until brown on each side, basting with the marinade from time to time. 15 minutes.

BROILED SALMON STEAKS

- An application of lemon juice adds greatly to the flavour of broiled salmon steaks. About an hour before cooking, brush both sides of each steak with lemon juice, cover loosely with waxed paper, and place in the refrigerator. When ready to cook, dust with flour, salt, and pepper. Then place on the grill.

RABBIT SARDINE PIE WITH STUFFED GREEN PEPPER AND WITH ONION CUSTARD
Serves 4

1 baked pie shell
2 cans sardines, drained

10 ounce can condensed cheese soup
⅓ cup milk

- Place sardines on bottom of pie shell
- Blend milk and soup
- Pour over sardines
- Bake in 350°F. oven 15-20 minutes
- Serve with stuffed Green Pepper and with Onion Custard (Page 190).

SCALLOP KABOBS
Serves 4

2 packages frozen scallops,
7 ounces each, or
1 pound fresh scallops

24 fresh mushrooms or water chestnuts
8 slices bacon

- Thaw scallops slightly, and take 8 small bamboo skewers.
- Thread 3 scallops and 3 mushrooms or water chestnuts alternately, putting a bacon slice in between.
- The bacon may be wound over one scallop and mushroom or cut into small pieces.
- Broil 5 minutes on each side or until bacon is crisp.
- Arrange two skewers for each serving on hot rice. Pour curry sauce over each serving, sprinkling with slivered almonds.

Streamlined Curry Sauce

1 can condensed cream of
chicken soup

½ cup chablis or other white wine
1 tablespoon curry powder

- Mix and heat slowly, stirring constantly until almost to a boil, simmer a few minutes.

COQUILLES ST.-JACQUES
Serves 4

1 pound sea or bay scallops
¼ cup butter or margarine
1 shallot, finely chopped or 1 small
white onion, chopped

¼ pound sliced fresh mushrooms
¼ teaspoon pepper
¼ cup dry white wine
bread crumbs

- Cut scallops in quarters, or thirds for the small ones.
- Simmer in butter with shallot or onion and the mushrooms 2-3 minutes over medium heat.
- Add wine and cook only a minute or two more.
- Put in the scallop shells or a small casserole and sprinkle top with bread crumbs. Dot with butter and bake in 500°F. oven for 3 minutes. Serve immediately.

MACARONI SHELLS STUFFED WITH SHRIMP   Serves 6

4 ounces large sea shells
  (pasta macaroni shells)
1/3 cup chopped celery
1/3 cup chopped onion
3 tablespoons vegetable oil
1 cup cottage cheese
1 7-ounce can shrimp, drained and cut
1 10-ounce package frozen spinach,
  cooked, drained, chopped
1 egg, slightly beaten
1/3 teaspoon salt

1/8 teaspoon oregano
1/8 teaspoon lemon juice
1/8 teaspoon pepper
3 tablespoons chopped onion
2 tablespoons vegetable oil
3 tablespoons flour
1/8 teaspoon salt
1 1/2 cups milk
1 chicken bouillon cube
3/4 cup water
1/3 cup grated Parmesan cheese

- Cook macaroni shells according to package directions, drain and rinse with cold water, drain well, chill.
- Cook celery and onion in hot oil only until tender; drain.
- Combine with cottage cheese and next 7 ingredients, mix well.
- Fill macaroni shells with shrimp mixture.
- In a saucepan cook onions until tender, blend in flour and salt.
- Stir in milk and chicken broth and stir and cook until thickened.
- Stir in cheese.
- Pour 1/2 of the sauce into a 12 x 7 x 2 inch casserole dish. Arrange stuffed shells in two layers in the sauce.
- Cover and bake in 375°F. oven for 15 minutes.
- Sprinkle remaining sauce on top and bake uncovered an additional 10 minutes.

SHRIMP AND COD WITH LEMON RICE   Serves 8

1 1/2 cups uncooked regular rice
2 teaspoons ground turmeric
1 teaspoon mustard seeds
1/2 cup butter or margarine
1/2 pound fresh or frozen shrimps,
  shelled and deveined
2 1 pound packages frozen cod or
  other white fleshed fish fillets

7 ounce can or jar pimientos,
  drained and diced
3/4 teaspoon salt
1 cup dry white wine
3 tablespoons lemon juice

- Cook rice according to package directions.
- Heat turmeric and mustard seeds in butter in a large frying pan 2 to 3 minutes. Stir in shrimps; sauté 5 minutes; remove with a slotted spoon and place in a 3 quart casserole.
- Cut frozen fish into chunks; cook, turning once or twice, until fish flakes easily, about 10 minutes. Add to casserole.
- Stir rice into drippings in pan; heat slowly, stirring constantly, until golden. Stir in pimientos and salt; spoon into casserole.
- Mix wine and lemon juice in a cup; stir into rice mixture. Cover; chill.
- Before serving, place dish, covered, in 350°F. oven for 1 hour and 15 minutes.

CURRIED SHRIMP

Serves 6

2 tablespoons butter or margarine
1 onion, chopped fine
⅓ cup chopped green apple
⅓ cup chopped celery
2 tablespoons curry powder

1 cup chicken broth or water
1½ pounds uncooked shrimp,
peeled and cleaned
1 cup cream
salt and pepper

- Cook onion, apple, celery, and curry powder in the butter briefly. Add broth or water, simmer until tender and the liquid has been reduced.
- Add cream and uncooked shrimp.
- Simmer gently until cream is slightly reduced and shrimp a pale pink. Serve over hot cooked rice.

BAVARIAN STYLE SMELTS

Serves 6

2 pounds smelts, fresh or
frozen
1½ cups beer
vegetable oil

¾ cup flour
¾ teaspoon salt
½ teaspoon pepper
lemon wedges

- Split, clean and remove heads from fresh smelts, or thaw frozen smelts. Pour beer over smelts in a large bowl; cover with transparent wrap; chill at least 1 hour.
- Pour in enough oil to make a 1 inch depth in frying pan; heat to 375°F.
- Combine flour, salt and pepper. Remove smelts from beer with a slotted spoon; reserve beer. Roll smelts in seasoned flour; dip again in beer, then again in seasoned flour.
- Fry smelts, 5 minutes or until golden, turning once. Lift out; drain on paper toweling. Serve immediately with lemon wedges.

DELUXE BAKED SOLE

Serves 4

1 pound sole fillets
3 tablespoons butter or margarine
salt and pepper

4 tablespoons finely chopped shallot
4 tablespoons parsley, chopped
¼ cup white wine or dry vermouth

- Simmer shallot, parsley and wine 5-7 minutes or until slightly reduced.
- Arrange fish fillets in a shallow baking dish and season with salt and pepper, dot with the butter, pour over the sauce, and bake in a 325°F. oven 5 minutes or until the fish is opaque and flakes when touched with a fork.

TUNA PUFF
Serves 4

2 cups mashed potatoes
2 7 ounce cans tuna, drained and flaked
4 eggs, beaten
⅓ cup grated Parmesan cheese

2 tablespoons fine dry bread crumbs
1 envelope white sauce mix
water
1 tablespoon lemon juice
dash seafood seasoning

- Combine potatoes, tuna, eggs and cheese in a large bowl.
- Butter a 1 quart casserole, then sprinkle with crumbs. Fill with potato mixture.
- Bake in 350°F. oven 1 hour, or until puffy and golden brown.
- Prepare white sauce mix in a small bowl, according to directions. Add lemon juice and seafood seasoning, blending well.
- Serve separately to spoon over tuna puff.

SWISS-TUNA SCALLOP
Serves 4

2 cups coarsely crushed saltines
1½ cups cream-style corn
7 ounce can tuna, drained and flaked
8 ounce package Swiss cheese shredded

¼ cup diced pimiento
1 cup milk
2 tablespoons butter or margarine
1 tablespoon minced onion

- Combine first 5 ingredients in a large bowl.
- Combine milk, butter or margarine and onion in a small saucepan; heat slowly until butter melts.
- Pour over tuna mixture; toss lightly. Spoon into a greased 1½ quart casserole.
- Bake in 350°F. oven 45 minutes.

TUNA CHOW MEIN CASSEROLE
Serves 4

¾ cup chopped celery
⅓ cup chopped onion (optional)
2 tablespoons chopped green pepper (optional)
1 tablespoon butter or margarine
1 7 ounce can tuna
½ (5½ ounce) can chow mein noodles (save ¼ cup)

10 ounce can condensed cream of mushroom soup
¼ cup milk
¼ cup water
⅛ teaspoon pepper

- In a large frying pan cook and stir celery, onions and green pepper in butter only until tender.
- Stir in tuna with liquid and the remaining ingredients and pour into ungreased 1½ quart casserole.
- Sprinkle with reserved chow mein noodles and bake in 350°F. oven 30 minutes.

TUNA-CHEESE IMPERIAL   Serves 6

8 ounce package wide noodles, cooked
½ cup butter or margarine
5 tablespoons flour
¾ teaspoon salt
¼ teaspoon pepper
2½ cups milk

1 8 ounce package cream cheese
1 7 ounce can tuna, drained
½ cup sliced pimiento-stuffed olives
2 tablespoons cut chives
1 6 ounce package sliced Muenster cheese
1½ cups bread crumbs

- Melt 5 tablespoons of the butter in a medium size saucepan; stir in flour, salt and pepper; cook, stirring constantly, until bubbly.
- Stir in milk; continue cooking and stirring until sauce thickens and boils, 1 minute.
- Slice cream cheese into sauce; stir until melted, then add tuna, olives and chives; remove from heat.
- Pour about ¾ cup of the sauce into a greased 2½ quart casserole, then layer other ingredients on top this way:
- Half of the noodles, half of remaining sauce, 2 slices Muenster cheese, remaining noodles, half of remaining sauce, remaining Muenster cheese and remaining sauce.
- Melt remaining butter in a small saucepan; add bread crumbs; toss lightly with a fork. Sprinkle over mixture.
- Bake in 350°F. oven 30 minutes, or until bubbly.

TUNA FLORENTINE CASSEROLE   Serves 8

4 tablespoons butter or margarine
1 onion chopped
¼ cup flour
½ teaspoon salt
dash nutmeg
2 cups milk
1½ cups process Gruyère cheese, shredded

2 7 ounce cans tuna, drained and flaked
2 10 ounce packages frozen chopped spinach, thawed and drained
½ cup fine dry bread crumbs
⅓ cup grated Parmesan cheese

- Melt butter in a medium-size saucepan; sauté onion only until soft; stir in flour, salt and nutmeg; cook, stirring constantly, until bubbly, stir in milk, continue cooking and stirring until sauce thickens and bubbles 1 minute; remove from heat. Stir in shredded cheese until melted; add tuna.
- Place spinach in the bottom of a lightly greased 1½ quart casserole; spoon tuna-cheese mixture over the top; top with crumbs and Parmesan cheese.
- Bake in 350°F. oven 25 minutes, or until golden.

TUNA RING WITH CHEESE SAUCE

Serves 4

1 egg
7 ounce can tuna, drained
¼ cup chopped onion
¼ cup Cheddar cheese, shredded
    (1 ounce)
¼ cup chopped parsley

½ teaspoon celery salt
⅛ teaspoon pepper
1 cup Biscuit type mix
¼ cup cold water
    Cheese sauce (recipe below)

- Beat egg slightly, set aside 2 tablespoons of this egg.
- Stir tuna, onion, cheese, parsley, celery salt and pepper into the remaining egg.
- Stir Biscuit Mix and water to a soft dough and knead 5 times on a floured board and roll into a rectangular shape.
- Spread tuna mixture over top. Roll up, beginning at the long side jelly-roll fashion with sealed edges down and then shape into a ring on a greased baking sheet. Pinch ends together.
- With scissors make cuts ⅔ of the way through at 1 inch intervals.
- Turn each section on its side to show the filling.
- Brush top with reserve egg.
- Bake in 375°F. oven for 25-30 minutes.
- Serve with hot cheese sauce.

HURRY-UP RICE SKILLET SUPPER

Serves 4

2 cups frozen mixed vegetables
2 tablespoons instant minced onion
2 cups water
1 can condensed cream of celery
    soup

1⅓ cups packaged precooked rice
7 ounce can tuna, drained
2 tablespoons dried parsley flakes
½ teaspoon leaf majoram, crumbled
1 teaspoon lemon juice

- Cook frozen mixed vegetables with onion and water in a large frying pan 5 minutes.
- Stir in soup until well blended. Add rice, tuna, parsley and marjoram. Mix to blend; heat slowly to boiling, stir constantly.
- Cover pan; lower heat. Simmer 5 minutes, or until rice is tender and mixture is creamy. Sprinkle with lemon juice.

BROILED SEAFOOD STEAK WITH ANCHOVY BUTTER

Serves 4

1½ pounds salmon, swordfish or
    halibut steak
3 tablespoons butter or margarine
2 tablespoons anchovy paste

2 teaspoons lemon juice
1 tablespoon finely chopped chives
    or parsley

- Brush the steak lightly with butter on both sides and place under a broiler 5-10 minutes on each side, or pan-broil on the top of the stove.
- Mix the rest of the butter with the anchovy paste, lemon juice, and chives, and pour on top of the hot steaks.

FISH AND BROCCOLI AU GRATIN   Serves 4

2 10 ounce package frozen broccoli
3 tablespoons butter or margarine
4 tablespoons flour
1¼ cups whole milk
1 cup grated Cheddar cheese

¼ cup sherry
salt and pepper to taste
2 pounds fish fillets (sole, halibut,
  salmon, or perch), frozen or fresh
paprika

- Cook broccoli according to directions on package, drain thoroughly.
- Melt butter and stir in the flour.
- Add milk and cook until mixture is smooth and thick, stirring constantly.
- Add cheese and stir over low heat until melted, add sherry and seasonings.
- Arrange broccoli on the bottom of a greased, shallow baking dish —
  (8 x 12 x 2 inches).
- Thaw fish fillets, lay over broccoli, cover with sauce, dust with paprika.
  Bake in 375°F. oven 25 minutes.

BOUILLABAISSE GOES MODERN   Serves 4

1 pound frozen fish fillets
  (haddock, cod, perch, etc.)
1 can cream of mushroom soup
28 ounce can tomatoes
1 cup cooked shrimp

1 pint fresh or frozen oysters
¼ cup sherry
½ teaspoon dried saffron
1 frozen King crab or ½ pound clams
  in their shells

- Put the fillets, soup, and tomatoes in a pan. Simmer over a low flame
  about 15 minutes, add the shrimp, saffron, oysters, and sherry.
- Cook 5 minutes, add crab or clams, warm and serve.

HOMEMADE FISH CAKES   Serves 4

1½ pounds raw or frozen fish fillets,
  thawed, chopped
1 onion chopped
2 eggs

2 tablespoons oil
¼ green pepper, chopped
3 tablespoons bread crumbs
salt and pepper

- Mix ingredients, shape into fish cakes, fry.

COLD SOUP SUPPER   Serves 4

1 quart buttermilk
2 cups diced cucumbers
⅓ cup chopped green onions,
  tops and bottoms
¾ cup diced, cooked cold beef,
  chicken, or flaked fish

1 cup cooked shrimp or crab or lobster
½ finely chopped dill pickle
¼ cup chopped parsley
2 hard-cooked eggs, sliced
salt and pepper

- Chill all ingredients together for two to three hours or more, except the
  egg.
- Serve very cold in large shallow soup bowls with an ice cube in each dish.
- Float several slices of egg in each bowl. Sprinkle with more parsley.

EASY FISHERMANS STEW

Serves 6

½ pound sliced bacon or ham
   trimmings
6 finely diced potatoes
4 onions, chopped fine
1½ pounds fresh or frozen fish,
   cut into 1½-2 inch pieces

1 cup catsup
salt, pepper, Tabasco sauce, and
   crumbled, dried red peppers

- Cut bacon into small pieces, brown slowly in a large pot or Dutch oven until crisp.
- Add potatoes and cook until tender, stirring constantly.
- Add onions when the potatoes are partly tender.
- Place the fish on top of the potatoes and onions, cover with water, add seasonings.
- Gently stir mixture to avoid breaking fish. More catsup may be used if desired.

SEAFOOD NEWBURG

Serves 6

3 tablespoons butter or margarine
3 cups cooked seafood (shrimp,
   crab flakes, mussels, oysters, etc.)
1 teaspoon paprika
½ teaspoon nutmeg
2 tablespoons flour

3 egg yolks
1 cup light cream and ½ cup milk
¾ teaspoon salt
¼ cup sherry
1 loaf unsliced bread
¼ cup melted butter or margarine

- Melt butter in a heavy frying pan, add flour, stir 2-3 minutes over low heat but do not brown. Add seafood, paprika, nutmeg.
- Beat the egg yolks with milk and cream, add to mixture slowly and cook over low heat, stir with wooden spoon until thickened, do not boil.
- Add salt and wine slowly so it will not curdle.
- Meanwhile, with a sharp knife cut off top of loaf of bread and outside crust. Cut the inside in a box fashion without cutting through, leaving walls ½ or ¾ inch thick.
- Brush inside and out with melted butter. Bake in 450°F. oven 10-15 minutes, or until brown. Fill with hot Newburg. Serve at once.

SALADS, SANDWICHES, EGGS AND CHEESE AROUND THE CLOCK

Serve lunch at dinner!

Salads and sandwiches, eggs and cheese are classically enjoyed at lunchtime or as an accompaniment at dinner.

Salads and sandwiches, eggs and cheese can be your dinner too, when a few extra touches are added.

Try Baked Potato Salad — a hot version of the old favourite potato salad, that includes wieners and cheese.

For sandwich style dinners, try Steak Heros or Hot Tuna Heros.

You'll find all are geared to good nutrition, good taste and a careful shopper.

Turn lunch into dinner some night soon.

TIPS ABOUT SALAD SANDWICH INGREDIENTS

- Don't wash away savings, remember don't wash salad greens until you're ready to use them.
- Tomatoes and cucumbers get moldy and rot.
- Lettuce turns rusty and gets limp. Take only as much lettuce as you're going to need for your salad. Then wash and dry it, so dressings will cling to the leaves.
- For a change of pace in salads, along with a vitamin A boost, use escarole, chicory and spinach instead of lettuce.
- As another lettuce-and-tomatoes alternative, consider making your own coleslaw. Cabbage is reasonably priced and goes a long way. Use half for coleslaw, half for cooked cabbage and several outer leaves for rolled cabbage dinner.
- For further salad variety, look for the less familiar regional or seasonal greens. A few examples are: head lettuce, spinach, lettuce escarole, romaine, endive, chinese lettuce, swiss chard and beet greens. You can cook these greens, of course, but don't miss out on the unusual flavor touches that just a few, chopped up, will add to a salad.
- Save on salad dressings by making your own.
- Save on mayonnaise and salad dressing by buying the quart size. It's thriftier than two pints, even for the small family. Buy when your favourite brand is on sale — you may save as much as 10 to 20¢ a quart.
- Pick out fairly firm, medium-size heads of lettuce, for larger ones may be overgrown and tend to be slightly bitter. If you spot a reddish discoloration at stem end, don't be concerned, for this is nature's way of sealing the cut that was made when the head was picked.
- As a general rule, you can count on about 4 servings from a medium-size head of lettuce, or 1 pound of loose greens, or a 1½-pound head of cabbage.
- For cost-cutting on sandwiches, try slicing cheese yourself and buying luncheon meats unsliced.

MONEY-SAVING CHEESE TIPS

Cheese (except cottage, cream and Neufchâtel cheeses) tastes best when served at room temperature. Remove from refrigerator about 30 to 60 minutes before serving. However, cut off only what you plan to use; wrap and return the remainder to the refrigerator. Warm air dries out cheese.

Remember two points when cooking with cheese: Use low heat and avoid overcooking.

Cheese and eggs offer good protein for very low cost. In addition they can be used in an unlimited number of ways for breakfast, lunch or dinner, and, any time in between.

Eggs alone can be made into a nutritional main course and they can be fried, baked, poached, soft boiled or scrambled.

Add a leftover and you've got the base for a tasty omelet.

Add cheese and you've got the base for casseroles, soufflés and blintzes.

Don't limit eggs to breakfast and cheese to lunch, Mix and Match — try one of these recipe ideas.

To find the relative cost of various cheese, compare the price of equal weights of cheese. As a general rule, you'll find aged or sharp natural cheeses usually cost more than mild ones; imported cheeses frequently cost more than domestic ones; pre-packaged, sliced, cubed or grated cheeses may cost more than wedges or sticks. Large packages are usually your thriftiest buy.

Save small or end pieces of cheese for garnishes. If the pieces become hard and dry, grate them and refrigerate in a covered container.

If mold appears on natural cheeses, scrape it off. It's harmless and does not affect the taste of the cheese.

Try cottage cheese and chives as a change from sour cream as a topping for baked potatoes. It's less expensive and has fewer calories.

MONEY-SAVING EGG TIPS

- What determines the price of eggs? Weight, among other things. For example: One dozen eggs in a carton marked EXTRA LARGE must weigh, according to government standard, 2¼ oz. per egg, those marked LARGE, 2 oz. per egg, MEDIUM, not less than 1¾ oz., but less than 2 oz.; and SMALL, not less than 1½ oz. but less than 1¾ oz. Weight is not listed on the carton, but the size is and that's your guarantee.

- How to figure cost per serving: Divide 12 into the cost per dozen. For example, if a dozen eggs cost 90¢, each egg actually costs 7.5¢. Therefore, an average 2-egg serving will cost you only 15¢. Nutritionists say that in buying a dozen large eggs at 90¢, the shopper is paying 60¢ a pound; for high quality protein; eggs are a bargain.

- Egg Grades: Most supermarkets carry Grade A Extra Large, Grade A Large and Grade A Medium eggs. All have the same nutritive value regardless of the size of the egg. A Grades are perfect for poaching, frying and cooking in the shell and, of course, are the higher priced than other grades.

- When checking the prices of eggs of the same grade, but different size, keep this formula in mind. If the difference in the price per dozen between medium and large eggs of the same grade is 7¢ or more, the medium size is the better buy per pound. If the difference is 6¢ or less, the larger size egg is the better buy.

- Brown shell eggs versus white shell eggs. Both have the same nutritional quality and, depending on size, should be priced comparably. The colour is determined by the breed of hen. Brown shell eggs are preferred in some parts of our country; white shells, in other regions. Smart shoppers buy either or both.

Money Saving Egg Tips (continued)

- Do not wash eggs until you're ready to use them, otherwise you remove the shell film that helps keep them fresh. Store them in the refrigerator as soon as you come home from the store. The tote-home carton is fine for storage and provides a light covering. If you change the eggs to a special compartment in your refrigerator, place them large end up.

- If an egg is ruined because of improper cooking, it's money thrown away. Whatever your favorite way of cooking eggs, use low heat.

- Eggs tend to be most plentiful and thus lower in price during the winter. So wintertime is often a time to think of main dishes from eggs.

- To save egg whites. Keep them chilled in a covered jar in the refrigerator. They will keep from 7 to 10 days. Beat whites with sugar until stiff and use as a garnish for puddings.

- To save egg yolks. Place them in a covered jar with just enough water to cover; chill. Plan to use them within 2 to 3 days. Or poach the yolks right away, then rice them and use for garnished salads. You can also hard-cook the yolks and store in a covered container for 4 to 5 days. Hard-cooked they're perfect mixed with mayonnaise, as a sandwich filling.

- The 2 egg omelet is one of the easiest, thriftiest ways to use any leftover meats, cheeses and vegetables.

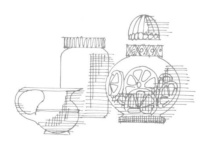

⇝EGG SECTION⇜

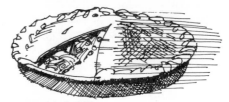

CORNED BEEF AND EGG PIE
Serves 6

1½ cups chopped onions
2 tablespoons butter or margarine
2½ cups chopped cooked corned beef
3 cups chopped boiled potatoes
2 teaspoons Worcestershire sauce

½ teaspoon salt
¼ teaspoon pepper
Pastry for 2 crust pies
¼ cup milk
6 eggs

- Sauté onion in butter until soft, about 5 minutes.
- Combine corned beef, potatoes, onions, Worcestershire sauce, salt and pepper.
- Roll out ½ of pastry to a 12-inch round on a lightly floured board; fit into a 9-inch, deep pie plate. Trim any crust overhang to ½ inch.
- Spoon beef mixture into prepared pastry shell, mounding centre higher than sides.
- Scoop a hollow about 1½ inches wide, 1 inch in from edge all around. Drizzle milk over hash.
- Break eggs into hollow, spacing evenly.
- Roll out remaining pastry to an 11-inch round; cut several slits near centre to let steam escape; cover pie.
- Trim overhang to ½ inch; turn edge under, flush with rim; flute edge. Brush top with milk.
- Bake in 450°F. oven 10 minutes, reduce heat to 400°F., bake 15 minutes longer, or until pastry is golden. Cut into wedges, serve hot.

CRUNCHY BAKED EGGS
Serves 4

4 slices bacon, diced,
  cooked until crisp,
  drained
2 cups cornflakes, crumbled
8 eggs

¼ teaspoon salt
⅛ teaspoon pepper
1½ tablespoons grated Parmesan
  cheese

- Coat cereal crumbs in frying pan in 1½ tablespoons bacon drippings.
- Grease 4 large custard cups (8-10 ounces).
- Sprinkle bacon in bottom of each.
- Press cereal crumbs around sides to form a nest.
- Slip eggs (2 into each cup) into nests.
- Sprinkle with salt and pepper.
- Bake in 375°F. oven for 8-10 minutes.
- Sprinkle with cheese and bake 5-7 minutes longer.

EGGS BAKED IN CHEESE SAUCE

Serves 4-6

¼ cup butter or margarine
¼ cup flour
3 cups milk
1 cup grated Cheddar or Swiss cheese
¼ teaspoon Worcestershire sauce

8 eggs
paprika
chopped parsley
8 slices toast

Make Sauce:

- Melt butter in saucepan, gradually stir in flour, continue stirring over low heat until mixture is bubbly.
- Gradually stir in milk, bring to a boil, stir and simmer 5 minutes.
- Remove from heat, add ½ cup cheese and Worcestershire sauce.
- Pour into a buttered 12 x 8 x 2 inch buttered casserole.
- Break 1 egg at a time into a saucer and slip into hot sauce. DO NOT CROWD.
- Top with remaining cheese.
- Bake in 350°F. oven for 20 minutes or until eggs are set.
- Sprinkle with paprika and parsley.
- Serve on toast.

EGGS SUBLIME

Serves 4

1¼ cups mushroom soup
4 softly poached eggs
2 tablespoons butter or margarine
2 tablespoons flour

⅓ clove garlic, finely chopped
⅓ cup milk or half-and-half
2 eggs, separated
½ cup grated sharp cheddar cheese

- Put ½ cup of the mushroom soup in the bottom of each of four individual au gratin dishes and place a poached egg on each.
- Melt the butter in a small saucepan and sauté garlic briefly.
- Add the flour, cook a minute or two, then add milk, slowly stirring until smooth and thickened.
- Add grated cheese, stir, remove from the fire, add egg yolks, blend well, and fold in stiffly beaten egg whites.
- Pile gently on each dish on top of the poached egg and mushroom mixture, spreading to the edges with a light and easy hand.
- Put in a 350°F. oven 25-30 minutes or until the top puffs up and springs back when lightly touched.

FLUFFY OMELET WITH CHEESE SAUCE   Serves 2

3 tablespoons butter or margarine	4 eggs separated
3 tablespoons flour	2 tablespoons water
½ teaspoon salt	dash of pepper
1 cup milk	1 tablespoon green pepper,
4 wedges process Gruyère cheese,	chopped
shredded	

- Make cheese sauce: Melt 2 tablespoons of the butter in a small saucepan; add flour and ¼ teaspoon of the salt. Cook over low heat, stirring constantly, until bubbly.
- Remove from heat; stir in milk slowly.
- Cook, stirring constantly, until sauce thickens and bubbles, 1 minute. Remove from heat; stir in cheese little by little until melted and smooth. Cover; keep warm.
- Beat egg whites in a large bowl until stiff.
- Beat egg yolks in a small bowl with remaining salt and pepper until thick and lemon-colored; beat in water. Fold into egg white mixture until no streaks of yellow remain.
- Heat a 9 inch frying pan or omelet pan with ovenproof handle.
- With a fork, swirl remaining butter or margarine over bottom and sides.
- Pour in egg mixture. Cook over low heat 5 minutes, or until mixture is set on the bottom and is golden-brown.
- Bake in 350°F. oven 10 minutes, or until puffy and lightly golden on the top.
- Loosen omelet around edge with a knife; lift onto heated large serving plate.
- Cut a gash with a knife down centre of omelet; sprinkle green pepper over one half.
- Spoon about ¾ cup of the cheese sauce over omelet; fold over with spatula. Spoon remaining sauce over the top. Serve at once.

GREEN PEPPERS WITH ONION CUSTARD

4 large green peppers with tops	3 egg yolks, slightly beaten
cut off and seeds and	1½ cups milk
membrane removed	salt and pepper to taste
1 onion, chopped	½ teaspoon Worcestershire sauce

- Heat milk, add to beaten egg yolks, onion, salt, pepper, and Worcestershire sauce, pour into peppers, set peppers in a small baking dish, close enough together so that they will stand up.
- Pour water into bottom of dish until it is ½ inch deep. Bake in 325°F. oven about 20 minutes or until custard is done.

ONION, EGG AND POTATO CAKE — Serves 4

2 tablespoons butter or margarine
1¼ cups peeled diced, raw potatoes
6 eggs
3 tablespoons water

¾ teaspoon seasoned salt
⅛ teaspoon thyme
1½ tablespoons chopped parsley
   or parsley flakes

- Melt butter in 9 inch frying pan or omelet pan. (Use one with removable or heat resistant handle)
- Add onion and potato, sauté, stir until potatoes are tender about 10 minutes.
- Beat eggs with remaining ingredients until blended but not frothy.
- Pour over onion and potato mixture.
- Cook slowly, as eggs set, lift with spatula to all uncooked portions to run underneath.
- When eggs are almost set on top place under broiler (6 inches from heat) for 1-2 minutes.
- Turn out, without folding, onto heated serving platter.

SAUSAGE AND EGG CREOLE — Serves 4-6

½ pound sausages cut into
   1 inch pieces
2 8 ounce cans tomato sauce
⅓ cup chopped green pepper
2 tablespoons instant minced onion
8 eggs

½ cup milk
¼ teaspoon salt
⅛ teaspoon pepper
   buttered toast
   commercial sour cream (optional)

- Brown sausages in frying pan, pour off excess fat.
- Add tomato sauce, green pepper and onion, simmer 5-7 minutes.
- Beat together eggs, milk, salt and pepper, scramble in a buttered frying pan.
- Place on buttered toast and spoon sausage tomato sauce over top.
- Top with sour cream.

SAUSAGES WITH SHIRRED EGGS — Serves 6

6 to 8 cocktail sausages
2 teaspoons butter
1 cup canned tomato soup

1 tablespoon chopped parsley
6 eggs
   salt and pepper

- Cut sausages into ½ inch pieces and cook in hot butter for 5 minutes.
- Add tomato soup and parsley; pour into 6 individual baking dishes.
- Break 1 egg into each dish on top of sauce; season with salt and pepper.
- Bake in 350°F. oven for 15 minutes or until of desired doneness.

⇒ CHEESE SECTION ⇐

CHEESE CRESCENTS

1½ cups flour	3 ounces Cheddar cheese, shredded
2 teaspoons baking powder	¼ cup salad oil
½ teaspoon salt	½ cup milk

- Measure dry ingredients into a bowl, measure oil and milk.
- Pour all at once into flour mixture and stir until mixture forms a ball.
- Knead dough about 10 times.
- Roll into a circle between two sheets of waxed paper about ½ inch thick.
- Cut into wedges, roll up, beginning at wide edge and place on hot meat mixture.

CHEESE SAUCE

2 tablespoons butter or margarine	1 cup milk
2 tablespoons Biscuit mix	2 ounces grated cheese
dash salt and pepper	

- Melt butter or margarine over low heat, blend in Biscuit Mix, salt and pepper.
- Cook slowly, stirring until smooth and bubbly.
- Remove from heat and stir in milk. Bring to boil, stirring constantly.
- Boil and stir 1 minute.
- Stir in cheese until melted.

MACARONI, CHEESE AND WIENERS   Serves 6

2 cups ready cooked macaroni, cooked, drained	⅛ teaspoon pepper
2 tablespoons butter or margarine	8 ounce package Swiss cheese, grated
3 tablespoons flour	1 pound wieners, cut into 1¾ inch pieces
⅓ teaspoon dry mustard	Paprika
3 cups milk	
⅓ teaspoon salt	

- Melt butter, add flour and mustard, cook for a few minutes, stirring constantly.
- Add milk gradually, stirring until smooth and thick.
- Add salt, pepper and ½ of the cheese, stir until cheese is melted.
- Stir in cooked macaroni and wieners.
- Place in 2-quart casserole dish and top with remaining cheese and sprinkle with paprika.
- Bake in 375°F. oven 30 minutes.

MACARONI'N CHEDDAR PUFF   Serves 6

1 cup uncooked elbow macaroni
6 tablespoons butter or margarine
6 tablespoons flour
2 teaspoons dry mustard
¾ teaspoon salt

1½ cups milk
1½ tablespoons Worcestershire sauce
1½ cups grated Cheddar cheese
6 eggs, separated

- Cook macaroni, following package directions; drain; cool.
- Melt butter in a medium size saucepan; stir in flour, mustard and salt; cook, stir constantly, until bubbly.
- Stir in milk and Worcestershire sauce; continue cooking and stirring until sauce thickens and boils 1 minute.
- Stir in cheese until melted; remove from heat. Let cool.
- Beat egg whites just until they form soft peaks.
- Beat egg yolks until creamy thick; beat in cheese sauce very slowly. Fold in egg whites until no streaks of white remain; fold in macaroni.
- Spoon into a greased 2 quart soufflé dish or straight side baking dish; gently cut a deep circle in mixture about 1 inch in from edge with a rubber spatula. (This gives the puff its high crown.)
- Bake in 300°F. oven 1 hour, or until puffy, firm and golden.
- Serve immediately .

TOASTY CHEESE BAKE   Serves 4

8 slices enriched white bread
  butter or margarine
½ pound ground beef
4 tablespoons chopped onion
2 tablespoons chopped celery
¾ tablespoon prepared mustard
½ teaspoon salt

2 ounces shredded Cheddar cheese
1 egg, slightly beaten
¾ cup milk
½ teaspoon salt
¼ teaspoon pepper
⅛ teaspoon dry mustard

- Toast bread and butter on both sides.
- Cook and stir the meat, onion and celery with prepared mustard and salt until the meat is brown and the onion is tender.
- Alternate layers of toast, meat mixture and cheese in a greased baking pan 9 x 9 x 2 inches.
- Mix remaining ingredients and pour over layers in pan. Bake in 350°F. oven approximately 30 minutes.

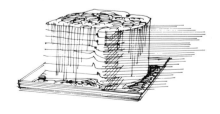

⇒ SALAD SECTION ⇐

BOEUF EN GELEE   Serves 6

3 medium carrots, pared, cut in
½ inch slices, cooked, drained,
chilled
1 pint Brussels sprouts, washed
and trimmed
2 cans condensed beef broth
1⅓ cups water

2 envelopes unflavored gelatin
3 tablespoons Madeira or dry sherry
6 drops Tabasco sauce
1 pound cooked roast beef,
sliced thin
watercress
horseradish Dressing (recipe follows)

- Combine beef broth and water in medium size bowl.
- Soften gelatin in 1 cup of broth, about 5 minutes, in a small saucepan.
- Heat, stirring constantly, until gelatin dissolves; stir into remaining broth in bowl.
- Add Madeira and Tabasco. Cut Brussels sprouts in half lengthwise.
- Pour ¾ cup of gelatin mixture into an 11 x 7 x 1½ inch pan or a 2 quart shallow mold; place in a larger pan of ice and water until gelatin is sticky-firm.
- Arrange part of the Brussels sprouts and carrots in decorative pattern along sides of pan.
- Make 12 rolls or bundles of meat slices; place 6 down center of pan, spacing evenly; spoon several tablespoons of remaining gelatin mixture over vegetables and meat.
- Arrange some of remaining Brussels sprouts against sides of pan.
- Add enough gelatin mixture to almost cover meat.
- Chill until sticky-firm.
- Arrange remaining meat and vegetables on top of first layer in pan; set pan on shelf in refrigerator; carefully spoon remaining gelatin over to cover meat and vegetables completely. Chill until firm.
- Just before serving, loosen gelatin around edges with a knife; dip pan quickly in and out of hot water; wipe off water.
- Cover pan with serving plate; turn upside down; shake gently; lift off mold.
- Border with watercress. Serve with Horseradish Dressing.

HORSERADISH DRESSING

- Combine ¾ cup salad dressing; 1 hard-cooked egg, sieved; 1 tablespoon tarragon vinegar; and 1 teaspoon prepared horseradish in a small bowl; stir to blend well. Cover; chill. Makes 1 cup.

MACARONI AND HAM SALAD   Serves 8

2 cups cooked elbow macaroni
2 cups cooked diced ham
⅔ cup chopped green pepper
⅓ cup chopped onion
¾ cup mayonnaise or salad dressing
½ teaspoon salt
⅛ teaspoon pepper
24 cherry tomatoes, halved

- Combine macaroni, ham, green pepper and onion in large bowl. Add mayonnaise, salt and pepper, toss to mix. Chill well.
- Just before serving, halve 1 cup cherry tomatoes, add to salad, toss lightly to mix. Garnish with remaining tomatoes.

POTATO, HAM AND EGG SALAD   Serves 8

5 medium size potatoes, peeled, cooked, diced
8 hard-cooked eggs, shelled, coarsely chopped
1 cup cubed Swiss cheese
1 cup cubed ham (or any leftover cold meat)
1½ tablespoons vegetable oil
½ cup chopped onion
2 tablespoons flour
1 tablespoon sugar
½ teaspoon salt
1 teaspoon dry mustard
1⅓ cups water
⅓ cup vinegar
½ cup chopped green pepper
¼ cup chopped pimiento

- Place potatoes in a 2½ quart casserole; add hard-cooked eggs and Swiss cheese.
- Brown ham; remove; reserve.
- Sauté onion in same pan until soft.
- Combine flour, sugar, salt and dry mustard; stir into drippings; cook, stirring constantly, until bubbly.
- Stir in water and vinegar; continue cooking and stirring until dressing thickens and bubbles 1 minute.
- Add green pepper and pimiento; cook 1 minute, pour over potato and egg mixture; toss lightly until combined; sprinkle with the reserved ham.
- Bake in 325°F. oven 10 minutes, or until mixture is hot.

SLICED MEAT IN ASPIC (HAM, TONGUE, CHICKEN)   Serves 8

sliced cooked chicken, tongue, turkey, or ham
2 tablespoons aspic jelly
1 cup boiling water
1 cup hot white wine
pimientos, cut in stars or hearts,
ripe olives, sliced and pitted

- Arrange any boned sliced meat in an overlapping and symmetrical design on a platter, chill thoroughly.
- Dilute aspic in the boiling water and white wine; chill until the consistency of unbeaten egg whites.
- Pour a thin layer over the chilled meat and chill until firm.
- If desired, decorate with hearts or stars cut with tiny cutters from whole pimientos, and make a design. Repeat with a second layer, softening the remaining jelly by heating if it becomes too hard.

HOT POTATO AND WIENER SALAD   Serves 4

4 large potatoes
1 pound wieners
2 tablespoons vegetable oil
1 cup chopped onion
1 large green pepper, halved,
   seeded, chopped

1 large red pepper, halved,
   seeded, chopped
1 teaspoon salt
¼ teaspoon ground pepper
⅓ cup vinegar

- Peel potatoes; cut into thin slices; cook in boiling salted water 15 minutes, or just until tender; drain well.
- Cut wieners into thin slices, brown in oil; push to one side; add onion; sauté until soft.
- Add chopped peppers, salt, ground pepper and vinegar; cook, stirring constantly, for about 2 minutes.
- Add drained potatoes to frying pan, toss gently to mix.
- Serve warm.

JELLIED MEAT LOAF (LAMB AND TONGUE)   Serves 8

2 pounds lamb shoulder and neck
   with bones, cut in chunks
   (or leftover leg of lamb)
2 lamb tongues or 1 veal tongue
1 onion, peeled and quartered
1 stalk celery

chopped bay leaf
1 clove garlic, chopped
salt and pepper
¼ cup chopped fresh parsley
2 envelopes plain gelatin

- Cook lamb shoulder, tongue, onion, celery, bay leaf and garlic in water until tender, (at least 1 hour).
- Remove from liquid, separate meat from bones; skin tongue and dice both meats, season with salt and pepper.
- Strain the liquid and measure.
- Add a mixture of water and white wine to make three cups.
- Put a layer of meat in a mould, sprinkled with chopped parsley, repeat until all the meat is used.
- The top layer should be meat; soften gelatin in a half cup broth which has been cooled, add to the balance of the liquid, heat and stir until dissolved.
- Pour over the meat in the mold, tipping to make sure that it seeps through all parts, and chill until firm. Unmold and slice.

PATE STYLE ASPIC

Serves 8

2 tablespoons gelatin
¼ cup white wine
2 cups canned, jellied consomme
1 pound liverwurst, softened, skinned

4 tablespoons butter or margarine, softened
⅛ teaspoon each nutmeg, salt, pepper
1 cup sour cream

- Soften gelatin in wine, heat soup, stir in the wine and gelatin, stirring until dissolved.
- Cool to lukewarm, pour one cup of soup into chilled 1 quart mold, tip it around so that it coats all the sides, chill 10-15 minutes, and repeat until the coating on the mold is about ½ inch deep.
- Mash liverwurst with butter and seasonings, until smooth.
- Add 1 cup of the soup and the sour cream, pile into the coated cold mold.
- Put mold in refrigerator.
- Before serving, unmold onto a small cold platter.

HAM, CHICKEN AND CHEESE LOAF

Serves 8-10

2 envelopes unflavored gelatin
½ cup cold water
½ teaspoon salt
⅛ teaspoon pepper
2 teaspoons grated onion
1 tablespoon lemon juice
1 cup boiling water

½ cup salad dressing
1 cup dairy sour cream
½ cup crumbled Roquefort or blue cheese
2 cups diced cooked ham
2 cups diced cooked chicken
1 cup finely chopped celery

- Soften gelatin in cold water. Add salt, pepper, onion, lemon juice and boiling water; stir until gelatin is dissolved.
- Add salad dressing, sour cream and cheese; stir until smooth.
- Chill over ice and water, stirring constantly, until as thick as unbeaten egg white.
- Fold in ham, chicken and celery; turn into a 9 x 5 x 3 inch loaf pan.
- Refrigerate until firm, about 3 hours.
- Garnish with salad greens and radish roses.

HEARTY CHICKEN SALAD

Serves 4

4 cups diced cooked chicken or turkey
1½ cups cooked green beans
1½ cups cooked carrots, cut julienne
2 boiled potatoes, sliced

2 cooked beets
¾ cup chopped onion
chopped fresh parsley

Dressing

3 tablespoons wine vinegar
3 tablespoons olive oil

salt and pepper
1 drop steak sauce

- Mix the sauce together and arrange the chilled vegetables and chicken in a bowl or platter.
- Pour dressing over, toss lightly to mix.

MADE FROM SCRATCH TUNA/CHICKEN SALAD   Serves 4

3 pound broiler-fryer
4 cups water
1 small onion, sliced
few celery tops
1/4 teaspoon salt
1/3 cup mayonnaise or salad dressing
1/3 cup dairy sour cream

1 1/2 tablespoon lemon juice
1/4 teaspoon pepper
1 cup chopped celery
1/2 cup chopped onion
1/2 cup grape halves
lettuce

- Place first 5 ingredients in a kettle or Dutch oven.
- Heat to boiling; reduce heat; cover; simmer 1 hour, or until chicken is tender. Remove from broth, cool.
- Skin chicken, take meat from bones.
- Cut meat into bite-size pieces; place in a bowl — or use 2 7-ounce tins tuna chunks.
- Combine celery, onion and grapes with chicken or tuna; add dressing; toss until evenly coated; cover; chill for at least 1 hour.
- Line salad bowl with lettuce leaves. Spoon salad into bowl.

TOSSED CHICKEN SALAD   Serves 6

3 pound broiler-fryer chicken
2 cups water
3/4 teaspoon salt
1/4 teaspoon pepper
1 cup chopped onion
Few sprigs of parsley
1 4 ounce can pimiento, drained, chopped
1 small clove of garlic, finely chopped

1/4 cup vegetable oil
1/3 cup catsup
2 tablespoons vinegar
1 tablespoon prepared mustard
1/2 teaspoon salt
1/2 teaspoon leaf rosemary, crumbled
1 cup uncooked regular rice
2 1/2 cups frozen peas, cooked
romaine leaves, broken

- Place first 6 ingredients in a large kettle or Dutch oven; bring to boiling; reduce heat; cover.
- Simmer 45 minutes, or until chicken is tender; remove chicken from kettle; cool; strain broth; reserve.
- Remove meat from bones; cut into bite-size pieces. Place chicken in a large bowl with pimiento and garlic.
- Stir oil, catsup, vinegar, mustard, salt and rosemary until well blended; pour over chicken; toss and cover, let stand at room temperature to season.
- Cook rice following package directions, using reserved chicken broth for part of the liquid. Cool.
- Add cooked peas and rice to chicken; toss lightly. Serve on romaine leaves.

SALAD NICOISE   Serves 6

5 medium size potatoes, cooked,
   drained, cooled
½ pound fresh green beans, cooked,
   drained, cooled
½ cup vegetable oil
⅓ cup wine vinegar
2 cloves garlic, crushed
1 tablespoon prepared mustard
1 tablespoon chopped parsley
½ teaspoon instant minced onion

¾ teaspoon salt
¼ teaspoon ground pepper
2 large tomatoes, sliced
1 red onion, diced
1 small green pepper, seeded, diced
6 ripe olives, halved (stone removed)
3 hard-cooked eggs, shelled, sliced
1 2 ounce can anchovy fillets, drained
2 medium size heads romaine
2 7 ounce cans tuna fish, drained

- Peel potatoes, cut into thick slices. Place in a shallow dish.
- Place beans in a second shallow dish.
- Combine rest of ingredients in a jar with a tight-fitting lid; shake well.
- Drizzle ½ cup over potatoes and 2 tablespoonfuls over beans; let each stand 30 minutes to season.
- Layer vegetables, eggs, anchovies and romaine in a large salad bowl.
- Break tuna into chunks; arrange on top. Pour rest of dressing over; toss lightly.

SALMON MOUSSE   Serves 6

2 envelopes unflavored gelatin
2 cups water
¼ cup lemon juice
1 envelope or teaspoon instant
   vegetable broth
   16 ounce can pink salmon

1 cup finely chopped celery
½ cup finely chopped seeded red pepper
2 tablespoons chopped parsley
3 tablespoons grated onion
½ teaspoon salt
¾ cup mayonnaise or salad dressing

- Soften gelatin in 1 cup water. Heat, stirring constantly until gelatin dissolves; remove from heat, cool, stir in 2 tablespoons lemon juice. Measure out ¾ cup of mixture and reserve.
- Stir remaining 1 cup of water and instant vegetable broth into remaining mixture in saucepan. Heat, stirring constantly until hot.
- Drain salmon and flake, removing bones and skin. Combine with celery, red pepper, parsley, grated onion, salt and mayonnaise. Stir in the ¾ cup gelatin mixture. Reserve while preparing mold.
- Pour half the remaining gelatin mixture into bottom of a 1½ quart fish shape mold; place in a large pan of ice and water; let stand turning mold often from side to side to form a thin coat of gelatin on bottom and sides of mold.
- Spoon salmon mixture over gelatin coated mold, spreading to cover mold completely. Chill in refrigerator until firm. When ready to serve, run a thin blade knife around top of salad, dip mold very quickly in and out of hot water. Cover with a chilled serving plate, turn upside down, shake gently, lift off mold. Garnish with cucumber slices and red pepper slices and service with mayonnaise.

⇒SANDWICH SECTION ⇐

BEEF BARBECUE SANDWICH   Serves 8

4 cups diced cooked beef
5 tablespoons butter or margarine
2 onions, diced
1 green pepper, diced
2 celery stalks, sliced
3 cups catsup
¼ cup Worcestershire sauce

⅓ cup lemon juice OR
⅓ cup dry red wine
¾ teaspoon salt
1 teaspoon Tabasco sauce
  dash allspice
½ teaspoon garlic powder
8 slices whole wheat bread

- Sauté onion, green pepper and celery in butter.
- Add 1 cup of water and all remaining ingredients except beef and bread, simmer 30-35 minutes.
- Add beef, simmer 10 minutes.
- Serve on whole wheat bread toasted or on toasted rolls.

GOURMET SUPPER SANDWICHES   Serves 6

⅓ pound sliced bacon, cooked,
  crisp
1 pound chicken livers
3 tablespoons chopped onion
1 3-4 ounce can sliced
  mushrooms
1 teaspoon salt

2½ teaspoons Worcestershire sauce
3 tablespoons butter or margarine
3 medium size tomatoes, sliced thin
2 teaspoons sugar
¼ teaspoon pepper
¼ cup chopped parsley
12 slices rye bread

- Stir chicken livers and onion into 2 tablespoons bacon drippings into pan.
- Cook slowly, stir constantly, until browned; stir in mushrooms and liquid, ¼ teaspoon of the salt, and Worcestershire sauce.
- Cook, stirring several times, until liquid evaporates. mash mixture well with a fork.
- Melt butter in a jelly-roll pan; place tomatoes in a single layer in pan; sprinkle with sugar, remaining salt and pepper.
- Heat in 350°F. oven 5 minutes, or until hot; sprinkle with parsley.
- Place each of 6 slices of bread on a serving plate; top with tomatoes, then drizzle buttery drippings from pan over tomatoes.
- Spread liver mixture over tomatoes, dividing evenly.
- Top with bacon and remaining bread slices.
- Cut each sandwich in half; serve hot with chips and dill pickles.

GRILLED STEAK SANDWICH

2 tablespoons chopped chives
1 tablespoon butter or margarine

4 small fillet steaks, ¼ inch thick
4 hamburger buns

- Mix chives with melted butter. Place steaks on grill and brush frequently with butter-chives mixture.
- A few minutes before the steaks are done, toast bun halves on the grill.
- Butter buns and serve steaks between the halves.

ISLAND SANDWICH   Serves 6

8-10 wieners, finely chopped
¼ cup chopped green pepper
¼ cup chopped cucumber
1½ tablespoons slivered almonds, toasted

¼ cup mayonnaise
¾ teaspoon lemon juice
¾ teaspoon Worcestershire sauce
¼ cup catsup
6 wiener rolls, split

- Combine all ingredients except rolls.
- Spread into split buns.
- Wrap each in foil.
- Bake in 400°F. oven 10-12 minutes.
- Serve with milk drink or dessert.

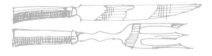

MEATBALL SANDWICHES   Serves 8

2 eggs beaten
3 tablespoons milk
½ cup dry bread crumbs
½ teaspoon salt
⅛ teaspoon pepper
1 pound ground beef
½ pound bulk sausage meat
¾ cup chopped onion
½ cup chopped green pepper

1 cup water
1 cup tomato sauce
¾ cup tomato paste
2 teaspoons sugar
½ teaspoon garlic powder
½ teaspoon oregano
½ teaspoon parsley flakes
8 crusty rolls

- Combine first 6 ingredients thoroughly and form into 24 (1½ inch) meat balls.
- Brown on all sides, remove.
- Add next 3 ingredients to pan and cook until sausage is brown, remove excess fat.
- Add next 7 ingredients and stir in meatballs; cover, simmer 15-20 minutes (stir occasionally).
- Remove top crust from rolls, scoop out centre and fill each with 3 meat-balls and sauce.

PIZZA STYLE SANDWICH   Serves 6

14 ounce package Pizza Mix
½ cup (3-5 slices) salami, finely diced
½ cup (3-5 slices) boiled ham,
  finely diced
½ cup (3-5 slices) bologna, finely diced
½ cup grated Mozzarella cheese
½ cup cottage cheese

- Combine flour and herbs from pizza mix and prepare according to package instructions.
- Roll dough on waxed paper 18" x 8" (rectangle).
- Combine all ingredients except pizza sauce.
- Spread evenly in dough.
- Roll up (jelly roll fashion) cut into 3 inch rolls.
- Place rolls seam side down on greased cookie sheet.
- Bake in 425°F. oven 12 minutes.
- Heat Pizza sauce and serve hot with rolls.

TURKEY ROUND-UP   Serves 6

½ cup salad dressing
1½ tablespoons chopped dill pickle
2 teaspoons finely chopped onion
12 slices Vienna or French style bread
6 1 ounce slices Swiss cheese
6 slices tomato
6 1 ounce slices salami or bologna
6 2½ ounce slices cooked turkey
6 tablespoons butter or margarine,
  softened

- Combine first 3 ingredients and spread on one side of bread slices.
- Top six bread slices with cheese, tomato, salami and turkey.
- Top with remaining bread slice.
- Spread butter on outside of sandwich. Grill slowly 10-12 minutes.

STEAK HEROS   Serves 4

3 medium size onions, peeled,
  sliced thin
2 medium size green peppers, seeded,
  sliced into thin rings
3 tablespoons butter or margarine
4 cube steaks, ¼ inch thick
4 hero rolls
2 medium size tomatoes,
  each cut in 8 slices
½ teaspoon salt
½ teaspoon pepper

- Sauté onions and green peppers in ½ tablespoon of the butter until soft; remove and keep warm.
- Sauté steaks in same frying pan 2 minutes on each side, or until done as you like.
- Split rolls almost through; open out flat. Spread with remaining butter; place on serving plates.
- Place tomato slices and steaks on rolls; sprinkle with salt and pepper.
- Spoon onion mixture over steaks. Serve hot with chips and a beverage.

MOCK REUBENS   Serves 4

28 ounce can sauerkraut
1 tart apple, halved, cored, diced
2 tablespoons sugar
¾ pound sausage links
1 tablespoon butter or margarine

½ cup mayonnaise or salad dressing
¾ cup chili sauce
1 teaspoon instant minced onion
½ cup grated Cheddar cheese
8 large slices caraway rye bread

- Drain liquid from sauerkraut; combine sauerkraut with apple and sugar; heat to boiling; cover; simmer 15 minutes to blend flavours; drain.
- Split sausages lengthwise; sauté in butter until lightly browned in a medium-size frying pan.
- Blend mayonnaise with chili sauce, onion and cheese in a small bowl.
- Place 2 slices of bread on each of 4 serving plates; place spoonful of sauerkraut over bread, topped with sausages.
- Pour over cheese mixture. Serve hot.

LITTLE LEAGUE BURGER SANDWICH   Serves 8

1 pound ground beef
⅓ cup chopped onion
1 tablespoon all-purpose flour
¼ teaspoon salt
1 can condensed vegetable soup

½ teaspoon Worcestershire sauce
1 cup sour cream
8 hamburger buns, split, toasted, buttered

- Brown beef and onion, drain excess fat.
- Blend in next 4 ingredients and cook until bubbly.
- Stir in cream, beat 1 minute.
- Spoon onto bottom half of bun and replace top.
- Serve with relish, and crisp vegetables, milk and cookies.

TUNA HEROES   Serves 6

2 7 ounce cans tuna fish
¾ cup chopped celery
1 cup fresh peas, shelled
4 slices process Swiss cheese, cubed

¼ cup chopped parsley
¾ cup mayonnaise or salad dressing
6 hero rolls
3 tablespoons butter or margarine, melted

- Drain tuna; separate into small-size chunks.
- Add celery, peas, cheese and parsley; fold in mayonnaise or salad dressing.
- Cut a slice from top of each roll; hollow out inside, leaving a ½-inch-thick shell.
- Brush insides of shells with melted butter; fill with tuna fish mixture.
- Wrap each separately in foil.
- Bake in 400°F. oven 15 minutes, or until filling is hot.
- Serve hot with lemon wedge and ripe olives.

INDEX TO INDIVIDUAL RECIPES

207